MY STORY, GOD'S GLORY

A Story of Redemption

"Breaking the Chains of Bondage"

Shannon R. Wright

Surrender All

Shlit
Ps. 40:1-3

Dedication

For my incredible husband who has stuck with me through

everything we have encountered. He is the true definition of a man

in love. When he said, "Til Death Do Us Part" he really meant it.

Through all of this, the Lord has brought us not only closer to each

other, but closer to Him. With the Lord being the head of our

household, we were able to overcome.

Acknowledgments

First and foremost, to my Lord and Savior Jesus Christ who saved my marriage, my family and my life. To my best friend, Keiann Miller, who has always been there for me, never gave up on me, has always believed in me and supported me through my journey. To my mother-in-law, Sue Wright, who led me to The Lord. To my favorite teacher I had in middle school, Mrs. Kathy Wait, who has always been a positive influence in my life. For my daughters' Nana, Amada Hasty, who has welcomed me as her own and has been a mother-figure to me. And last but not least, Alison D. Nation for her incredible talents in creating my book cover. I told you what I wanted and you nailed it! You are awesome!

Introduction

I want to start off by telling you that I am not a preacher, an evangelist, or a Sunday school teacher. I don't claim to be perfect, I don't live a sinless life, and I am far from a saint. I was not raised in church and have absolutely no Theology background at all. I am just an ordinary 35 year old woman who lives in Tennessee with a Bachelor of Science Degree in Physical Education, and I am a certified Personal Trainer. I am a mother of two wonderful daughters and I have been married to the man of my dreams since 2002. The purpose of this book is to tell you that no matter who you are, what kind of life you have lived (or are living), what type of educational background you have or where you are from, Satan is seeking to destroy your life. But praise God! You have a Heavenly Father, a Master, a Comforter, a King, a Savior and Redeemer who is ready and willing to lead your life where He wants it to go. This book is a story of hope, and it was laid on my heart to write and show people who are hurting and lost that there is an answer and an end to all of your brokenness and pain.

Today I am healed and delivered from the brokenness, rejection, shame and strongholds of my past. But there are times I still struggle with guilt, shame and sadness. I have forgiven the people who have hurt me and rejected me. I love and pray for them every day. I live for an awesome God who has faithfully lead me to the purposeful life I live now with no regrets and no turning back. This is my story about a woman who had to be broken and lost before she could be found and put back together. I have purpose and passion for my life that I live for God, no longer for myself. I have dedicated my life to serving Him and helping women and married couples find hope in a hopeless world. I heard someone say, "Healed people, heal people." I hope my story of hope and redemption might heal your brokenness.

Psalms 18:16-19 (NIV) *"He reached down from on high and took*
hold of me;
he drew me out of deep waters.
He rescued me from my powerful enemy,
from my foes, who were too strong for me.
They confronted me in the day of my disaster,

but the Lord was my support.

He brought me out into a spacious place;

he rescued me because he delighted in me."

All you have to do is.......Surrender.

Chapter 1

Surrender Childhood Abuse

Growing up in a small town in Michigan we experienced cold winters and comfortable summers. I enjoyed snow sledding down hills of fresh snow and swimming in the Great Lakes. The best memory of my childhood was camping with my family. We would ride bikes, swim in the lake, enjoy hayrides, make s'mores and hot dogs over our campfire, and buy candy at the campground candy store. Those wonderful memories are forever engrained in my heart.

I have to laugh at people in the South, where I live now, when the news anchors threaten the chance of snow. People in the South rush to the grocery store in a panic buying milk and bread because they think that the storm of the century is coming and they will be shut in for a week! In Michigan, it was very rare to have a snow-day where we didn't have to go to school. As a former school teacher in Tennessee, I loved the threat of snow because that meant we weren't going to school that day.

My husband, children and I visit my family in Michigan twice a year; once at Christmas and the other during summer break. My kids love to sled in the snow and enjoy the beach at Lake Michigan. With my family living in Michigan and my husband's family living in Chattanooga we've spent a lot of time traveling on our summer and winter breaks.

I have wonderful memories growing up in Michigan, but I also have very painful memories as well. There are people who have said that a broken past doesn't affect a person's future; in my case that is a very big misconception - they have not walked a step in my shoes. Those people have not suffered from a painful past and were not forced to move on and live a normal life. The fact is, the bad things that happen to people become the root of future choices and behaviors. These are not excuses, they are reasons. There are people who have had a messy past who look for worldly things to satisfy their emptiness. Unfortunately, they look in all of the wrong places for happiness, as I did for so many years. I have spoken to women who had a similar past as mine and they masked their pain with alcohol, affairs, drugs, sex, and eating disorders.

To protect everyone involved, I will not be going into detail about all of the abuse I experienced and I will not be mentioning any names. The events that occurred are written to the best of my knowledge and memory. But just know, that if you are someone like me trying to get through a troubled present due to a painful past, there is hope!

Let me start out by telling you that I have been face down in the deepest pit anyone could imagine. And not only once, twice, or even three times. I have been in many pits, many times. But as my favorite scripture reads in Psalm 40:1-3, "I waited patiently for the Lord; he turned to me and heard my cry. He lifted me out of the slimy pit, out of the mud and mire; he set my feet on a rock and gave me a firm place to stand. He put a new song in my mouth, a hymn of praise to our God. Many will see and fear and put their trust in the Lord." (NIV)

I am sure many of you can relate to the pits you are currently in or have been in the past. Take heart, my friends, it is a long road but it does not have to be traveled alone. Just as recently as October 2, 2014, Jesus outstretched His arms to me in the deepest, darkest pit I had been in to date and asked, "Are you done trying to do it yourself? Are you finished leading a life that does not have me at the forefront? Are you ready to surrender your life to me and start to see the blessings begin to pour out for your life?" I was flat on my face crying out to Him desperately and yelled, "Yes! I surrender to You, Lord!" From that day on, I have never been the same.

The abuse I went through as a child and into early adulthood is an important part of who I am today. As with all of you, your past is part of who you are and who God wants you to be. Please remember, I am not glorifying the abuse I have experienced or the sins I have committed. But God is using me as a testimony to others to show that no matter what you have been through or the life that you have lived, it is not too late to repent of your sins, ask for forgiveness and follow Him. "If we confess our sins, He is faithful and just and will forgive us our sins and purify us from all unrighteousness." 1 John 1:9 (NIV)

There are many stories that I could tell you about the abuse I experienced as a child as well as through adulthood. But through the years I have learned to push them down deeper and deeper so I didn't have to face them. When I started going to counseling, my counselor told me that I had to face my past and take Jesus with me. That has been an extremely difficult process for me to do, and as I continue to do it today it has forced me to bring everything back up that I have pushed down for so many years. But I know that it will be a wonderful healing process in the end.

Abuse can be masked with money, gifts, nice houses, boats and campers, but a child would give it all back to hear an unconditional, "I love you" and "I am proud of you." One story from my childhood happened when I was about 12 years old on a sunny, summer day. I woke up early and ate my bowl of cereal. I played outside, went swimming in the pool and built up a hearty appetite ready to eat lunch. I was so hungry and I kept asking if I could have some lunch; by this time it was a good six hours since I had my breakfast. My abuser kept saying no. They became annoyed with me asking if I could eat lunch and that is when it happened. They yelled at me to get to the table and sit down. Taking everything out of the freezer, refrigerator, and pantry, it was all put on the table. The entire dining room table was full of food. They yelled, "You'd better eat everything on this table! You are not to get off that chair until everything on the table is gone! And if you throw up, you are going to eat that too!" I remember the look on their face and the sound of their voice screaming at me – it was like they were demon-possessed! But things like that happened all the time. I remember when I would ride the bus from school and wanted to hide in the back of the bus so I didn't have to get off the bus. I wanted to stay on the bus so the driver could take me home with her. Another incident was when I was 18 years old. One of my abusers grabbed me and threw me to the ground, got on top of me and started choking me; I could not breathe and I was so scared! They screamed in my face, "I swear to *** I am going to ******* kill you!"

The pit that lead to a life of destruction happened years ago as a child, and I just kept digging it deeper as the years went by. Growing up in a very abusive situation has lasting consequences that you are unaware of at the time. I did not realize that this treatment was not normal. I thought that behind every closed door this type of activity went on with everyone. My abusers told me multiple times in my life that I make it hard for anyone to love me; I was a mistake and they wished I'd never been born.

I was a tomboy who liked to wear baggy clothes, I developed a rebellious attitude, I didn't do well in school and was just very different from other kids. The attitude developed from the many mistakes and failures I went through that eventually led to insecurities that I will be discussing further in depth later in the book. It seemed like no matter what I did, it was never good enough. Over time, I developed an "I don't care" because it didn't matter, I wasn't going to please anyone anyway. So I took my pain and frustrations out on explicit rap music I felt I could relate to, used inappropriate language, had an encounter with police, lied, stole, cheated, began smoking (at the young age of 10) and if I could have gotten my hands on drugs and alcohol, I would have done that too. I would perform self-mutilation because the burning pain of the knives and razor blades actually felt good. I felt a lot of stress, pain and frustrations leaving my body.

As I said in the introduction, I am not without sin. Being saved and living for the Lord doesn't mean you won't have bad days; you will most definitely slip up, you are not insulated from sin, and you will experience pain and trying times in your life. But if the spirit of Christ is in you, you will not *want* to continue to sin. In 1 John 3:9 it reads, "No one who is born of God will continue to sin, because God's seed remains in them; they cannot go on sinning, because they have been born of God." (NIV) It also states in James 4:17 "So whoever knows the right thing to do and fails to do it, for him it is sin." When you allow God to lead you to do everything in your life, you will realize how lost you really were.

I have been at the lowest of the lows and have experienced the darkest of pits. But that is where I needed to be – I had to be lost in order to be found. I had to be broken in order to be put back together. Once I was so low that I couldn't get any lower, my only option was to look up. God wants us to completely rely on Him for everything. He wants to direct your life where He wants it to go. He wants your full attention and devotion to Him. He wants to bring himself glory by delivering you from your deep, dark pit.

I was not raised in church, I did not go to Sunday school and God was not talked about. I believed in God though, and I had heard that Jesus died on the cross for our sins, but as a child, I didn't comprehend what that meant. We prayed at the dinner table, a prayer that we had memorized, but there was no meaning behind it. When we went to bed at night we prayed another prayer that was memorized. The prayers were never explained to me and what the meaning of them were. As a young child and having no idea who The Lord was, I just thought He was a mythical figure who lived in the clouds. Praying was just a routine we did every day; it was a life based on works. As long as we were good people who didn't kill anyone, rob a bank or end up in jail, we would go to heaven. Of course, that is not true. Unfortunately, there will be a lot of good people in Hell who never asked Jesus into their heart.

I started going to church by myself when I was young; I was dropped off at church and picked up after the service was over. When I was old enough to date, I dated guys who attended church so I attended with them. When I was in college I went to a local church on my own because I always felt like it was the right thing to do. I listened to the sermons, but really didn't understand them nor did I have anyone to talk to about the meaning of the messages. So as my husband and I like to call it, I was just "playing church" for all of those years. God was a convenient God; we only went to Him when we really needed something selfishly.

In my very limited experience, religion seems to be different in the North than in the South. That shouldn't be the case because the God who people worship in the North is the same God people worship in the South. Anyway, I attended a couple different churches while living in Michigan. Of course, I had no idea what the differences in all of them were at the time. But in the North, I don't remember preachers talking much about getting saved, living your life for The Lord, repenting your sins, and completely turning your life towards God. I am not implying that they didn't, it just wasn't emphasized enough to really stick out in my memory. My understanding at the time was that if we just believed in God, that alone would be enough to get us into heaven. And if we were "good people" who lived a normal life (whatever that is) then we were saved and going to heaven. But when I moved down South with my husband, I experienced a whole new perspective on religion. I learned quickly that just being a "good person" and having good works alone does not get you into heaven. In Ephesians 2:8-9 it reads "For it is by grace you have been saved, through faith—and this is not from yourselves, it is the gift of God— not by works, so that no one can boast." (NIV) But again, I was a young person who didn't understand religion so that was just my perspective and recollection of it.

Jesus took our place on the cross that day on Calvary to bear our sins. We not only need to believe what He did for us, but we also need to live by His teachings throughout our life. "My son, do not forget my teaching, but keep my commands in your heart, for they will prolong your life many years and bring you peace and prosperity. Let love and faithfulness never leave you; bind them around your neck, write them on the tablet of your heart" Proverbs 3:1-3 (NIV).

My experience of conflict resolution was to yell and scream without anything being accomplished. I didn't know how to handle disappointments and failures. It was not OK to fail at anything; I had to be the best at everything. So when something went wrong, we would argue and fight until one of us felt like we won. We were too proud to admit we were wrong, so any type of reconciliation was not an option. As a mature, grown adult now, I see that does not work in raising a family and resolving conflicts. We all face storms and troubling times in our lives, but when The Lord is the head of the household, storms will be calmed when we seek His guidance. In 2 Samuel 23:5 "If my house were not right with God, surely he would not have made with me an everlasting covenant, arranged and secured in every part; surely he would not bring to fruition my salvation and grant me my every desire."

(NIV) In James 4, it states that people often quarrel and fight due to not submitting themselves to God and why being humble works better than being proud. We are all born with a selfish nature, we tend to live a selfish life that is paralleled to the scripture in James 4. Our motives selfishly appease our flesh. We naturally do not want to give up our sinful lives to live for God. Jesus states in the Bible that we must pick up our cross daily and follow Him. That means that we must die to ourselves and sacrifice a life that requires living for Him. "Submit yourselves, then, to God. Resist the devil, and he will flee from you. Come near to God and he will come near to you. Wash your hands, you sinners, and purify your hearts, you double-minded. Grieve, mourn and wail. Change your laughter to mourning and your joy to gloom. Humble yourselves before the Lord, and he will lift you up." I am here to tell you, ever since my life has been completely turned around by our Lord and Savior, my days of fighting and quarrelling are done. Don't get me wrong, we will have a disagreement every now and then and I get frustrated with my husband and children at times. But I have learned how to handle fights, disappointments, failures and disagreements much better now that I have peace in my heart and God as my defender. God saw my heart and my brokenness, and He turned a messed-up, confused, sad woman into a bold and devoted Christian. I am certainly aware of my past, but I am not shackled to it. I am a living example of one of my favorite scriptures, 2 Corinthians 5:17 "Therefore, if anyone is in Christ, he is a new creation; old things have passed away; behold, all things have become new." No matter what you have done, what other people have done to you, or what you have done to yourself, your past does not have to determine your future. Whether something or someone has affected your life thirty years ago or thirty minutes ago, God is willing and able to redeem your past and help you move forward into a flourishing life.

Before I close this first chapter out I want to reiterate a few things. First, God loves you no matter what you are going through or where you have been. He is waiting for you to turn your face to Him and follow his lead. Second, if you have experienced childhood abuse let me be the first one to tell you, it is not your fault. You were an innocent child who did not know any better than what you were taught and exposed to in your upbringing. You were just following the examples that were put in front of you; you are a product of your environment. At the same time, though, I am not saying that it is ok to go out and live a life of sin just because you had a rough childhood. I take full responsibility and ownership of what I have done. No one made me make the choices I made. That is the very first thing everyone must realize before healing can begin. I know many people who have not experienced any type of trauma in their life. They tend to state that an abusive past is no excuse for bad decisions that have been made. My response to that is simple; things happen to people. Sometimes those things are so detrimental to a person that it influences a person's life in the most negative ways for years after they take place. The truth is, those things are often the root of future choices and behaviors. Again, they are not excuses, they are reasons. They don't justify bad choices and behaviors, rather, bad choices and behaviors are manifested as ways to cope with the negative events that occurred in the past. I have a shameful past, and I have no problem stating that fact. It is not the past mistakes that we need to focus on, it is the cleansing and redemption of my past that we celebrate. I have a past that has been forgiven and transformed into something positive as a testament to God's grace and mercy for me and so many others. I share openly about what I have done, but more importantly, I share what God has done for me because it helps me to minister to people who have experienced similar circumstances. If you let Him, God will take over your life and lead you down a path that you will never want to detour from. There is hope in you just as there was hope in me. After 34 years I can finally see the light, and I never want to go back into darkness. If you have experienced any type of abuse that has affected your life, it does not have to take over your life one day longer. You will get through it. It won't be painless, quick or easy. But I am a living testimony that God will use your painful situation for good. All you need to do is surrender it to Him.

We know that we will not live a sinless life, but we need to live a blameless life. Because we are human and we have been born into sin, we all sin. So we must not judge others for their sins when we have our own. Because Jesus died on the cross for the forgiveness of our sins, we must forgive others of their sins and wrong doings. If we do not forgive those who have done us wrong then God says that we are storing up wrath against ourselves and we will never experience peace and freedom from the binding we have to the unforgiveness that is pent up in us. We will never live perfect, sinless lives. The only one who has lived a perfect, sinless life is our Lord and Savior Jesus Christ himself. To be a Christian means "Christ-like'; in other words, to be a Christian you want to live a life that portrays the image of Christ. The Christians of the world need to live lives that are forgiving and loving just as the Lord forgives and loves us each day. In 1 John 1:5-10 it talks about how we should live in the light and not in darkness when we become Christians and how we must forgive others as Jesus forgives us. "This is the message we have heard from him and declare to you: God is light; in him there is no darkness at all. If we claim to have fellowship with him and yet walk in the darkness, we lie and do not live out the truth. But if we walk in the light, as he is the light, we have fellowship with one another, and the blood of Jesus, his Son, purifies us from all sin. If we claim to be without sin, we deceive ourselves and the truth is not in us. If we confess our sins, he is faithful and just and will forgive us our sins and purify us from all unrighteousness. If we claim we have not sinned, we make him out to be a liar and his word is not in us." (NIV)

The people who have hurt me in the past, I have truly forgiven. I love them and pray for them every day. I know they may not have meant to do and say what they did, but I ask The Lord every day for them to see how their actions have affected lives, and I pray that their hearts become softened. I know it could've been worse, and it could've also been better. I understand that different people handle different situations in different ways. But however each person handles the life that has been given to them, it will affect them in some way through their journey of life.

Here are some scriptures to help comfort the abused:

> • Romans 8:4-16 "For those who are led by the Spirit of God are the children of God. The Spirit you received does not make you slaves, so that you live in fear again; rather, the Spirit you received

brought about your adoption to sonship. And by him we cry "Abba, Father." The Spirit himself testifies with our spirit that we are God's children." (NIV)

• John 10:10 "The thief comes only to steal and kill and destroy; I have come that they might have life, and that they might have it more abundantly." (NIV)

• Psalm 9:9 "The Lord is a stronghold for the oppressed, a stronghold in times of trouble." (NIV)

• Psalms 34:18 "The Lord is near to those who have a broken heart, and saves such as a contrite spirit." (NIV)

• Psalms 147:3 "He heals the brokenhearted and binds up their wounds." (NIV)

Chapter 2

Surrender Unforgiveness

Matthew 18:21-22 says, "Then Peter came to Jesus and asked,

"Lord, how many times shall I forgive my brother or sister who

sins against me? Up to seven times?" Jesus answered, "I tell you,

not seven times, but seventy-seven times." (NIV) That verse

continues on to speak about the unmerciful servant who is the only

one imprisoned and tortured in the end due to not forgiving the

person who wronged him. (Matthew 18:33-34) So you can see that there is a monumental price for unforgiveness that will enslave you. I understand that it is difficult to continue to forgive those who have sinned against you - trust me I know! It is especially hard to forgive someone that you loved and trusted dearly and can't believe they would do something like that to you. But just as Jesus says in the above scripture, not only do you forgive them one time, but seventy-seven times. Forgiving someone who has hurt you is an extremely difficult, lengthy process. It is not as easy as it sounds. If you are anything like me you have anger, bitterness, hurt, betrayal, broken trust, and confusion. The list goes on and on. So before you can start the process of forgiving someone, you must work through the underlying issues first. Why did this person do this to me? What did I do to deserve this? Those are very valid questions that have sought-after answers.

Along with unforgiveness comes anger. Anger is a natural reaction to someone who has badly hurt you. If you want to experience true healing, you must let go of the anger. God wants us to not only let go of our anger, but to forgive those who have hurt us. In an area of our life where we have been so hurt, it is difficult to imagine ourselves letting go of anger and forgiving that person. But with God's grace, it is possible. Forgiveness is not forgetting. We don't "forgive and forget"; we don't imply amnesia. It is not minimizing the hurt saying, "It's ok, it didn't hurt that much." No, we were hurt and in my situation, I was hurt for many years. Forgiveness states exactly what has happened just as a referee states a call in a basketball game; it is what it is. Forgiving does not necessarily mean reconciliation. Forgiveness and reconciliation are two separate issues. We definitely need to forgive, but reconciliation is completely based on our situation. For example, a woman who is continually being physically abused by her husband is in danger of staying in that marriage. If she decides to end the marriage, she can forgive him but she does not need to reconcile with him because he has proven over and over that he is not a healthy person for her to have in her life. In my case, I have forgiven my abusers, but I have not reconciled with them. I tried to for many years, and they continued with the abuse. So I have cut all ties with them, and I am no longer exposed to the abuse I experienced for so many years. I live an extremely peaceful life now that they are no longer in my life, but I pray for their salvation every day. If they turn away from their lives of sin and give their hearts to God, I would consider reconciliation one day if it is The Lord's will. But for now, my walk with The Lord has grown tremendously since the day I cut all ties with them and truly forgave them.

In some situations, the person needing forgiveness may not be a saved person. Often they are prideful, arrogant, and think that the world owes them something and they do not owe anyone anything. Pride is Satan's specialty; it is the characteristic that most describes him. Pride is the issue that had him expelled from Heaven. Pride is still one of Satan's most successful tools in discouraging people from accepting the gospel of Jesus Christ. God hates pride.

People who are not saved do not have the peace in their hearts that they will receive when they surrender to The Lord. That was something that was difficult for me to understand for a long time. I am not taking away from the sins we have committed prior to being saved, but I do understand that it is not who we are. It is the devil who has a grip on us and will not let go until it is literally an act of God that delivers us from it. Until we turn from our sinful ways and truly sell out to God, we will always have bitterness, pride, and anger dwelling inside us. Once we are saved, our hearts are softened and our lives are changed almost immediately. When it becomes difficult to understand why we should forgive those people who have hurt and betrayed us in so many ways, we need to remember the verse from Proverbs 3:5-6 "Trust in the Lord with all your heart, do not depend on your own understanding. Seek his will in all you do, and he will show you which path to take." That scripture can be used in so many other facets of life; jobs, family, career, relationships and so on. Another verse that can guide you in the process of forgiving and transforming your life is Romans 12:2. "Don't copy the behavior and customs of this world, but let God transform you into a new person by changing the way you think. Then you will learn to know God's will for you, which is good and pleasing and perfect." God's word, through prayer and reading the Bible, helps you to overcome unforgiveness, anger, bitterness, and pride. It releases you from the stronghold it has on you that claims your happiness and replaces it with Christ-like thoughts and actions. When your relationship grows in Christ, He gives the gift of spiritual discernment and helps you to forgive those who have hurt you just as He has forgiven you for hurting Him.

I am not sure about your case, but in my case the abusers do not show evidence of being saved. They may believe in God but they do not attend church, walk in His ways, speak as a saved person or practice any type of religion whatsoever. The bible says that we will be known by our fruits. If there is no evidence of fruits, how will there be evidence of salvation? So it is my job as a Christian, who tries my best to live for the Lord every day, to forgive them as Jesus forgave me. Matthew 6:14-16 says, "For if you forgive other people when they sin against you, your heavenly Father will also forgive you. But if you do not forgive others their sins, your Father will not forgive your sins." (NIV) I know that it is the hardest thing you can do, but you will receive the most wonderful blessings you can imagine when you do forgive them. Just as I confessed my sins, repented and asked for forgiveness that lead to salvation, 1 John 1:9 states, "If we confess our sins, he is faithful and just to forgive us our sins and to cleanse us from all unrighteousness." (NIV) On the other hand, if you are having a difficult time forgiving someone in your life, you will have to pray *for* that person and that God leads them to repentance. God wants you to go to Him with everything, and that includes your stronghold of unforgiveness toward someone who has done you wrong. Now, this "forgiveness" thing sounds so easy, right? Nope! There is more to it, and I would like to dig deeper into scripture about forgiveness.

What does God require you to do to receive forgiveness from Him? He asks for a repentant heart that leads to salvation. In Luke 17:3 states, "If your brother or sister sins against you, rebuke them; and if they repent, forgive them." The Lord requires you to forgive someone only if they have repented of their sins and asked for forgiveness. Forgiveness is not required for someone who does not confess their sins, admit they did wrong, and come to you with a repentant heart. The same goes for us - if we don't go to The Father with a true repentant heart, if we don't turn from our sinful ways, He will not forgive us. Once the person or persons who sinned against you shows remorse for their wrongdoing, does everything to show how sorry they truly are, repents of their sins and completely turns away from that life of sin, only then are we instructed to forgive.

Unfortunately, my abusers haven't apologized for what they have done and they have never acknowledged what they did. In order for someone to receive the gift of salvation, they must first admit they are a sinner in need of a Savior. If people do not see they are sinners, they will not be repentant of their sins. People who are not Christians and who have not asked Jesus into their hearts or allowed Him to transform their lives, they live with hardened and selfish hearts. When people are saved, their hearts are softened. They will want to live as Christ-like as possible; however, this does not mean they will live perfect. Remember, the only perfect One is Jesus. They will not want to cause harm unto people, they do not want to use inappropriate language, they do not want to drink, steal, lie, gossip, cheat, fight, or do anything else that makes their Heavenly Father unhappy. They want to live for the Lord and testify to others what He has done for them. I want to shout from the rooftops how God has completely changed my life and has softened my heart in so many ways that when someone encounters me, I want the light of Jesus to shine through me onto them. Ephesians 2:8, "For it is by grace you have been saved, through faith—and this is not from yourselves, it is the gift of God." (NIV) Because of His gift of grace and salvation, He has softened my heart and made it possible for me to forgive.

If we do not learn to forgive, we will have spiritual barriers in our walk with God. We will have pent-up bitterness and it will make it hard for us to move on with life. We have to let it go and give it to God. Because we are human and naturally want to do things ourselves, we will never be able to forgive if we don't surrender control to God. Forgiveness is not for the person who has wronged you, it is to set you free from the bondage you will continue to live in. Trust me on this, you cannot live this life on your own. But remember, just because you forgive someone for their wrong-doing, does not mean you have to keep that relationship going. You can forgive someone and move on with life without having to keep them in your life.

True forgiveness is very seldom easy to do. It can be very costly, but it offers us a powerful weapon to break down the walls and strongholds in our hearts and lives. The enemy uses our strongholds of unforgiveness and anger to keep us in bondage. When we surrender our strongholds to Jesus, we set our hearts free so God can do things in our lives that we never thought possible!

Here are some scriptures on forgiveness to study:

• Ephesians 4:30-32 "And do not grieve the Holy Spirit of God, with whom you were sealed for the day of redemption. Get rid of all bitterness, rage and anger, brawling and slander, along with every form of malice. Be kind and compassionate to one another, forgiving each other, just as in Christ God forgave you." (NIV)

• Ephesians 4:25-27 "Therefore each of you must put off falsehood and speak truthfully to your neighbor, for we are all members of one body. "In your anger do not sin." Do not let the sun go down while you are still angry, and do not give the devil a foothold. (NIV)

• Romans 12:17-21 "Do not repay anyone evil for evil. Be careful to do what is right in the eyes of everyone. If it is possible, as far as it depends on you, live at peace with everyone. Do not take revenge, my dear friends, but leave room for God's wrath, for it is written: "It is mine to avenge; I will repay," says the Lord.

• Romans 12:20 "On the contrary, If your enemy is hungry, feed him; if he is thirsty, give him something to drink. In doing this, you will heap burning coals on his head." Do not be overcome by evil, but overcome evil with good. (NIV)

• James 1:19-21 "My dear brothers and sisters, take note of this: Everyone should be quick to listen, slow to speak and slow to become angry, because human anger does not produce the righteousness that God desires. Therefore, get rid of all moral filth and the evil that is so prevalent and humbly accept the word planted in you, which can save you." (NIV)

• Colossians 3:15-16 "Let the peace of Christ rule in your hearts, since as members of one body you were called to peace. And be thankful. Let the message of Christ dwell among you richly as you teach and admonish one another with all wisdom through psalms, hymns, and songs from the Spirit, singing to God with gratitude in your hearts." (NIV)

• James 3:14 "But if you harbor bitter envy and selfish ambition in your hearts, do not boast about it or deny the truth." (NIV)

Chapter 3

Surrender Insecurity

"You are a waste of skin! You should never have been born! No one is going to hire you, you are too stupid! You make it hard to love you! You will never amount to anything! You are nothing but a failure! It's all your fault!" If these words sound familiar to you, you are not alone. These are words that I heard from my abusers more than I would like to admit. I once heard that you don't need actual bruises to show abuse. Emotional abuse is extremely detrimental to anyone's self-worth, security, self-image and ability

to accept deep and sincere love someday. For those of us who have been wounded with abuse in our past and present, we build-up walls around us to protect ourselves from being hurt by anyone again. So when you finally do meet that special someone who really won't hurt you, it is difficult to let your walls down to let them in and truly experience the love they want to give you. After so many years of being told that you are unlovable, or only loved on conditions, it is extremely difficult to accept someone's love who is willing to give it to you unconditionally.

My husband is the greatest man I have ever known who has shown me unconditional love, next to Jesus of course. But due to my past, I can't let that love be fully absorbed the way that he wants it to. I have a very tall wall of bricks built up around me that will only take time, along with God's help, to take down. Each day a brick is taken down to eventually let him in to allow myself to experience the deep love he has for me. Don't get me wrong, we all have our problems in a marriage. He has hurt me and Lord knows I have hurt him. But when you are used to conditional love, it really makes it difficult to accept love without conditions.

My husband was raised with unconditional love shown to him. He did not have to "measure up" to any standard, love was not just shown to him by being the best athlete or bringing home good grades. He never had to worry about guarding his heart in fear of it being broken. But after the extremely traumatic event that happened in our marriage in the summer of 2014, which I will discuss later in the book, has changed him forever. It is now very difficult for him to let his walls down to love and really trust again. Though our love and passion for each other is stronger than it ever has been, due to the mistrust and betrayal, it is taking him a long time to break down his walls and allow himself to fully love me again. That makes me extremely sad, but I completely understand.

After surrendering my life to The Lord, I have realized that not only does my husband have unconditional love for me, but so does my Lord and Savior Jesus Christ. He loves His children unconditionally. Romans 5:8, "But God demonstrates his own love for us in this: While we were still sinners, Christ died for us." (NIV) God knows we are sinners and He knows we are going to sin before we even commit that sin. He hates the sin but loves the sinner. He still loves us through our faults and flaws, just as parents, for example, should love their children through their faults and flaws. We are not to love our children just because they played a great basketball game or because made an A on that Math test. We love them when they fail a test in school and when they score zero points in a game. Those are the times we should love them a little more.

Those of us who are young in Christ, and possibly life-long Christians, may have a hard time accepting that Christ could love and accept us for who we are; He wants us to come to Him just as we are. We have all committed sins, we have done stupid things in our lives that make us think, *"How could anyone love me for what I have done? I don't deserve this love. How could God, the creator of the world, love and forgive me? If anyone found out everything I have ever done, there is no way they are going to love me for me."* Trust me, I know how this feels – I have mastered the "stupid thing" routine. There are many days I think to myself that I am unqualified, unworthy, doubting God and everyone else could really love me for the person I was and the person I am now. But just as it says in 1 Corinthians 13:4-7, "Love is patient, love is kind. It does not envy, it does not boast, it is not proud. It does not dishonor others, it is not self-seeking, it is not easily angered, it keeps no record of wrongs. Love does not delight in evil but rejoices with the truth. It always protects, always trusts, always hopes, and always perseveres." (NIV) Jesus loves us just as we are.

We all have insecurities, whether it be the color of our hair or the number on the scale that we obsessively step on every day. Whatever it is, we all have something we are insecure about. My husband is insecure about his looks because he was teased as a child for his red hair, big chin, bow legs and his out-of-style clothes. My insecurities are not so much my looks but the way I perceive things. Because I was told for so many years that I would never amount to anything and could only be loved on conditions, the insecurities have manifested into adulthood, whereas my husband's have changed over the years due to his maturity in his looks and ability to purchase the clothes he chooses.

One insecurity I experienced as a child, among many of them, was the difficulty I had in school. I could not understand the material we were covering in class, no matter how long I studied for it. If a person spent an hour studying for a test or doing homework, it would take me three hours to do the same work. I had a learning disability that was extremely difficult to live with my entire educational years. I had to see a tutor once a week and attended Summer school. The kids in my class at school would always ask, "Why do you leave with that tutor all the time? What do you do with her outside the classroom?" Of course, I didn't want to tell the kids that I had a hard time with school work so I had to have extra help outside the classroom. The teacher would call on me in class to answer a question and I didn't know the answer, so the teacher would laugh at me along with the students in class. As a kid, that was detrimental to my psyche, and my life outside school only exacerbated it. I didn't receive the support and patience I feel I needed to succeed. So once again, those walls were built up around me to avoid letting anyone in.

Although there were no physical signs of any type of disability, from the emotional scars of the kids teasing me, to the hurtful fights I constantly had with my abusers, what I encountered was more than I could handle. The brokenness I felt on the inside from the label that was placed on me, drove my insecurity through adulthood that I continue to struggle with today. I hated going to school, I hated learning, I hated going to that special education classroom with that teacher, I hated myself, I hated my life!

If the abuse and insecurities a person experienced in childhood is not resolved, it will be brought into adulthood and into a marriage and family. When the simplest things are brought to my attention that I have done wrong or not well enough, I put up my wall in defense immediately. Of course, that is how I perceive it because that is all I have ever known. But to my husband, children and God, they do not see my shortcomings as failure because they know that no one is perfect and we all make mistakes. But to me, it brings me back to my childhood where I could never do anything right because no matter what I did, it was never good enough. After years of being told that, I built a wall around me so strong that the only person who can break it down is God.

Accepting that God loves us unconditionally has been an extremely difficult task for me along with many other people I have mentored. But once you experience His unconditional love and acceptance, you will feel a peace in your life that you have never felt before. In Jeremiah 31:3 it says, "The Lord appeared to us in the past, saying "I have loved you with an everlasting love; I have drawn you with unfailing kindness." (NIV) In Deuteronomy 7:7-8, "The Lord did not set his affection on you and choose you because you were more numerous than other peoples, for you were the fewest of all peoples. But it was because the Lord loved you and kept the oath he swore to your ancestors that he brought you out with a mighty hand and redeemed you from the land of slavery, from the power of Pharaoh King of Egypt." (NIV)

As Jesus hung on the cross he cried out to God about the Roman soldiers who nailed him there, "Father forgive them, they know not what they do." I don't know about you, but that is love that I could never comprehend. Jesus is asking God to forgive these men who abused him, spit on him, beat him, mocked him, shoved a crown of thorns on his head, and nailed him to the cross.

All because of the unconditional love he has for the world. There is no one else in this world who has that type of love for us. So instead of focusing on pleasing the people in your life, focus on pleasing God. Because if you are focusing on pleasing Him, then you won't have to worry about pleasing anyone else. We take a huge risk in life when we accept Jesus into our hearts and live a life pleasing to Him. The risk I have taken is losing some family members and possibly past friendships due to following Jesus. But it is a risk I have to be willing to take because as the bible says, these earthly people and things will surely pass away but God's words and promises will live on forever. It is God who we will have to face on judgment day where you will stand at the foot of His throne awaiting His ultimate judgment on you. At that time, it will no longer matter who you have pleased or displeased in your earthly life because no one will stand before Him with you except for you alone. The ultimate judgment we should all want to hear from The Creator of the world is, "Well done my good and faithful servant." Praise the Lord!

When people wear a label, it tends to be what they see when they look in the mirror. I could never see past my "disability" and depression. People, including myself, carry that feeling of not being good enough, being different than their peers, and believing the lies from Satan that no one will ever want to marry them. As a woman who is saved, redeemed and living for Jesus every single day, I still struggle with these feelings from my past. Because contrary to what people may believe, just because you are saved does not erase the pain and memories of what happened. It does, however, give us a safe place to go when our enemy tries to defeat us. Whatever your insecurities may be, be sure to lay them at the foot of the cross knowing that The Lord will take them up from you and cast them far away. You must stay in the word of God and pray every day for The Lord to lead you where He wants you to go. If you listen to Him, read The Bible, pray, ask for spiritual guidance for your life and follow His lead, you will never have to worry about pleasing anyone here on earth ever again. I tried for so long to gain acceptance and security from my earthly peers and all I ever did was fail. But once I realized that there is no one here on earth who deserves to have that kind of power over me and my life, it made life so much easier knowing that as long as I was pleasing The Lord, my days of fearing failure were diminished.

I had spent years searching for happiness and fulfillment for my life. I started business after business. I spent 10 years teaching as a career. I've rehabbed multiple real estate investments and have been an avid athlete and fitness guru for as long as I can remember. I had done all of this searching without God's guidance. I thought I could live this life on my own; it was *my* life and *my* choices. Oh friend, let me tell you, that is what led me down the road to nothing but heartache, financial loss, marital problems, insecurities and much more. I would have never imagined living the life I have been living since I gave up control and surrendered my life to The Lord; I never knew this kind of life existed. Yes, my husband and I still enjoy our real estate investments, which is a hobby we do together. It is a wonderful time for us to bond as a married couple. I still love fitness and continue to work out regularly; I have modified it from 60 hours a week to 6! But as The Lord changes my heart daily to grow closer to Him, I realize that this life of mine is not really mine. He is the potter and I am the clay. Where He leads me, I will follow. Because the life I lived, trying to please myself and others, was a life that was lived insecurely and was very tiresome.

I would like to end this chapter with text from a wonderful book by Tracie Miles called, "Your Life Still Counts: How God Uses Your Past to Create a Beautiful Future." I can relate to this passage all too well:

"Since everyone wants to feel loved and accepted, we all put up whatever defenses we think will help us stay safe. None of us want to feel ashamed, judged, or criticized. Nobody wants to feel inferior to the people around them. And if you have ever taken the risk of being real with someone and they shut you down or criticized you, you don't ever want to feel those emotions of hurt, betrayal, and shame again. As a result, you wear a mask that portrays the "you" that you are willing to let the world see. This mask does not form overnight. It begins

when we are just children and can get tighter and tighter as we age.

Maybe a parent, a grandparent, or parental figure made you feel ashamed of who you are, what you look like, what you've done, or how you act. Maybe someone hurt you when you were too young to defend yourself and left you feeling shattered or humiliated. Maybe you made a mistake in your life, and you are so ashamed of yourself, you can't imagine bearing the potential judgment of others as well. Maybe you are painfully insecure, so you try hard to wear a mask of confidence and never let anyone in, or you stay tucked away from others to protect yourself.

Each of us has a different reason why we put on a mask, and it's possible the sheer thought of being transparent and trusting others might make you tremble in your high-heel shoes. But God knows that when we remove our masks, we are in for a cornucopia of blessings. By taking a risk and learning to be real, we allow others the opportunity to love on us and pray for us, instead of denying them the opportunity to do so. We invite people into our lives to walk us through hard times, hard memories, and hard emotions instead of keeping everyone at arm's length. If we have overcome a certain adversity and experienced God's redemption and transformation, being real opens the door for us to be a vessel of hope to someone else in desperate need of a comforting touch from someone who truly understands.

There is power in being real because when we are real for God, God becomes real to other people. Understanding our value in Christ and believing we all have God-given potential are prerequisites to setting out on this journey to discovering how God can use our past for our purpose. Wearing a mask skews our view of God and what He wants to do in our lives. It inhibits us from living lives to our full potential and keeps us bogged down with the weight of trying to keep up the charade of what we want people to see. Only when we begin taking off our masks and being real with ourselves, God, and others can we truly discover peace and purpose."

Here are some helpful Bible verses to study that speak about pleasing The Lord and fulfilling His will for your life:

- 1 John 3:22 "And whatever we ask we receive from him, because we keep his commandments and do what pleases him." (ESV)

- Hebrews 13:16 "Do not neglect to do good and to share what you have, for such sacrifices are pleasing to God." (ESV)

- Romans 12:2 "Do not conform to the pattern of this world, but be transformed by the renewing of your mind. Then you will be able to test and approve what God's will is—his good, pleasing and perfect will." (NIV)

- Hebrews 11:6 "And without faith it is impossible to please him, for whoever would draw near to God must believe that he exists and that he rewards those who seek him." (ESV)

- Romans 8:5-8 "Those who live according to the flesh have their minds set on what the flesh desires; but those who live in accordance with the Spirit have their minds set on what the Spirit desires. The mind governed by the flesh is death, but the mind governed by the Spirit is life and peace. The mind governed by the flesh is hostile to God; it does not submit to God's law, nor can it do so. Those who are in the realm of the flesh cannot please God." (NIV)

• Proverbs 16:7 "When a man's ways please the Lord, he makes even his enemies to be at peace with him." (ESV)

• John 8:29 "And he who sent me is with me. He has not left me alone, for I always do the things that are pleasing to him."(ESV)

• Psalm 40:8 "I delight to do your will, O my God; your law is within my heart." (ESV)

• Colossians 1:9-10 "And so, from the day we heard, we have not ceased to pray for you, asking that you may be filled with the knowledge of his will in all spiritual wisdom and understanding, so as to walk in a manner worthy of the Lord, fully pleasing to him, bearing fruit in every good work and increasing in the knowledge of God." (ESV)

• 1 Thessalonians 2:4 "But just as we have been approved by God to be entrusted with the gospel, so we speak, not to please man, but to please God who tests our hearts." (ESV)

Chapter 4

Surrender Depression

"Why am I so sad all the time? Why does everyone else seem to be so happy?" These were questions that were so hard for my 13 year old mind to understand at the time. I did not have any guidance or education on mental health issues. I was never taught that what I was feeling was not normal. In fact, I was told the complete opposite. "Oh Shannon, stop being so dramatic! You are just doing that for attention! That is just part of being a kid and part of growing up!" So once again, I had to push all of those feelings down deep into my soul and just carry on. Feelings of rebellion, rejection, shame and anger were manifesting inside me already. Even as a child, the enemy was trying to destroy the plans God had for me in my life. He knew that I was going to be a force to be reckoned with, but even more, a powerful redeemed child of God doing His work for His Heavenly Kingdom in my future.

One day at school I found out about this new thing that people were doing to themselves, self-mutilation. They would take knives and cut themselves in places on their bodies that no one could see. It was a few days later when I was home by myself that I went to the kitchen and grabbed a steak knife out of the drawer and went into the bathroom. I will never forget the sting of that cold, sharp knife cutting through the skin on my arm. The pain from the knife cutting into my skin hurt so good, I didn't want it to stop. It felt as if my emotional pain and sadness were released through the cuts in my skin. My mind was focused on the painful cuts more than on my painful thoughts and emotions.

Eventually the cutting became a lot worse and I started cutting my face with razor blades. Once I started cutting places on my body that were visible, I started getting the attention from my parents. Shoot! What kind of story was I going to muster up for cuts on my face? I told my parents that my best friend and I were running through the halls at school and we tripped and fell and in the middle of my fall her ring cut my face..... *really, Shannon? Is that the best you could come up with?* Needless to say, that explanation did not go over too well. After many episodes of self-mutilation, fighting, crying, bringing home bad grades, and many more red flags, it was time for me to get professional help.

The first time I ever spoke to a counselor was like speaking to someone from a foreign country. I had no idea what to say, I had no idea how to say it. Again, I had no guidance or instruction on how to tell a complete stranger everything my 13 year-old messed up mind was thinking and doing. I never experienced that "safe place" to feel comfortable and welcomed to speak about everything I was struggling with. There were things that I had been doing that I did not want anyone to know about. It was never portrayed to me that it was OK to tell how I felt and that I would not be judged or thought of badly. We just needed to get down to the root of the problem; of course, that never happened. After weeks of failed attempts to see a counselor, we decided to give anti-depressants a try. Though they worked for a while, they were not the answer to my problem and not a long-term fix. Shortly after I stopped taking them, the flood of sadness continued. Depression followed me from childhood through my child-bearing years. If someone has never experienced depression, it can be explained as if you are wearing a blind fold, the skies you are seeing are constantly grey no matter how brightly the sun shines. It is like sitting in a dark room all alone and if you were in a busy crowd somewhere, you would still feel alone. It is a sadness that never goes away, no matter how hard you try. It does not matter what activities you are doing or the people you surround yourself with; you just want to be alone. You feel as if the world is closing in on you. I just wanted to go to sleep and never wake up.

My husband and I had our first baby, Maleah, May 17, 2006. She was a 7 pound, 10 ounce healthy baby girl. I had a Csection so it made my recovery & postpartum even more difficult on me. My husband and I had absolutely no idea what we were doing as new parents. I had never changed a diaper before, the baby cried all the time, she never slept through the night until she was over a year old, she had nine ear infections in the first year of life and the stress was really taking a toll on me. The day I brought Maleah home from the hospital was supposed to be a very happy and joyful day. But unfortunately, it didn't turn out that way. There were multiple events that happened the day we arrived home from the hospital and thereafter, that led to the darkest hole I had ever been in to date. From that point on I lived with severe postpartum depression for the next four years. I had terrible thoughts of killing my baby as well as myself; I was in a dark place that I could not escape. I was diagnosed with postpartum depression and bipolar disorder. The doctor prescribed medications for my disorders that had terrible side effects that made me feel like a walking zombie along with a weight-gain of 30 pounds in one month. With side effects like these, you can only imagine what my marriage started looking like. The intimate side of marriage was non-existent and quality time spent together was nowhere to be found. Our marriage was slipping through the cracks, one lonely day at a time.

My husband started researching natural ways to help with my postpartum depression and bipolar disorder. He came across an herbal medicine that could only be purchased from a company in Canada. Even though I had to take 15 pills a day, that medicine was a life and marriage-saver! I started taking the herbal supplement and my depression subsided and I was actually ready to have another baby! Four and a half years after our first baby was born, our wonderful 8 pound baby girl, Finley, was born. I remained on the herbal supplement for another 6 months after Finley was born because I was so scared that I was going to have to relive the postpartum all over again. But praise The Lord, I never experienced postpartum or bipolar disorder another minute of my life!

Here are some scriptures to help you or someone you know who is experiencing depression.

- Psalm 34:17-18 "When the righteous cry for help, the Lord hears and delivers them out of all their troubles. The Lord is near to the brokenhearted and saves the crushed in spirit." (NIV)

- Matthew 11:28 "Come to me, all who labor and are heavy laden, and I will give you rest." (NIV)

- 1 Peter 5:7 "Casting all your anxieties on him, because he cares for you." (NIV)

- Jeremiah 29:11 "For I know the plans I have for you, declares the Lord, plans for welfare and not for evil, to give you a future and a hope." (NIV)

- Psalm 30:5"For his anger is but for a moment, and his favor is for a lifetime. Weeping may tarry for the night, but joy comes with the morning." (NIV)

Chapter 5

Surrender Control

I find it interesting how *we* think that we are in control of our lives.
That we are going to make the decision about what we are going to
do because it is our life. Don't get me wrong, you need to make
plans for your life and how you will achieve goals and ambitions
for your future. You take your passions in life and pursue them
into a career and future for yourself. You may plan to have the
standard; two kids, a house with a picket fence, a dog and a cat,
and a job that you will work at for thirty years, and retire in Florida

with all of the other "Florida Snowbirds." Oh, but how life can throw you a curveball! Since middle school, I had always wanted to be a Physical Education (PE) teacher. My favorite subject in school was Physical Education, which was the only class where I ever received an A and experienced continued success.....pretty sad, huh? So I thought to myself, *since I love PE, everyone else loves it too, I want to teach it when I grow up!* After five years of college and a couple of interviews, I landed my first teaching job in August 2005. I should have listened to my gut-instinct the very first day of student-teaching in college. I knew right away that this job was not for me. Teaching Physical Education was very different than participating in it as a kid in class. But as all immature-minded kids think, if I like it, everyone else must like it. That was not the case at all. I never realized that not all kids enjoyed PE; who wouldn't like to play games and run around a huge room? I was a very athletic kid so I naturally loved it. But apparently, a lot of kids who do not like sports, do not like Physical Education class.

When I began teaching in 2005, I disliked my job so much that I started to search for different employment opportunities. I sent approximately 100 applications to various employers and did not receive one phone call for a job that would have been worth quitting my current teaching position. I remember my husband and I walking around our circle driveway at our home, pushing our oldest daughter in a stroller, discussing what our purpose was on Earth. We did not feel like we were contributing to the world and had no direction in our lives. We decided to start business after business. The first venture we started was a personalized gift business called Babies To Brides and it was a complete flop. Then I wanted to buy a women's fitness franchise business, but that fell through. Then I sold products for a multi-level marketing company for a while and spent more money than I made. Finally we started an embroidery and screen printing business that made us a lot of money, but it also brought us a lot of problems.

As I have stated before, my husband grew up in a family with a lot of unconditional love and acceptance shown to him, but not a lot of money. Whereas, I grew up in a financially comfortable situation, but was desperate for unconditional love and acceptance. Two people who came from two completely different backgrounds in need of two completely different things was just a train wreck waiting to happen. When the money started flowing in from the embroidery and screen printing business, the statement "more money, more problems" held true in our marriage. The business grew larger than we had ever expected. We started it when the real estate business was slow and the economy was down. When we saw that the embroidery and screen printing business was financially successful, we thought about working it full-time. The problem was, my husband and I did not have a passion for it. It was not enjoyable or sustainable. The thought of renting or purchasing a commercial building in town was not our heart's desire, we solely did it for the money. The problem with running a successful business, two full-time teaching positions, a growing fitness business, two children, and managing real estate investments was, how could we have possibly focused on our children and marriage? Where would we find the time? Well, we didn't, and that was where the problems started. You can't serve two masters, money and God, so we chose money. Matthew 6:24 states, "No one can serve two masters, for either he will hate the one and love the other, or he will be devoted to the one and despise the other. You cannot serve God and money." (NIV)

God will allow you to be brought to the point of surrendering to His Lordship. It is very different for different people. Some people are brought down quickly and easily, but for some people it may take a little more time and do a lot more damage; our situation was that of the latter. When my husband started allowing money to be his idol and fitness my idol, God had had enough and allowed Satan to enter our marriage in more ways than one. God makes it clear that we are not to have idols above Him. In Exodus 20:3 He states, "You shall have no other Gods before me."

After four years of the madness we were living in, the time came when I told my husband that enough was enough and I wanted to sell the business. It consumed us, it took over his life and started causing health problems as well as marital problems. He was sleeping on the couch and we were just business partners living under the same roof. But October 2013 was what really caught his attention!

One night he was sleeping on the couch and his heart went into atrial fibrillation, Atrial fibrillation (A-tre-al fi-bri-LA-shun), or AFib, is the most common type of arrhythmia. An arrhythmia is a problem with the rate or rhythm of the heartbeat. During an arrhythmia, the heart can beat too fast, too slow, or with an irregular rhythm. AFib occurs if rapid, disorganized electrical signals cause the heart's two upper chambers—called the atria (AY-tree-uh)—to fibrillate. The term "fibrillate" means to contract very fast and irregularly. In AFib, blood pools in the atria. It isn't pumped completely into the heart's two lower chambers, called the ventricles (VEN-trih-kuls). As a result, the heart's upper and lower chambers don't work together as they should. He remembers laying in the emergency room hospital bed while the doctors shocked his heart back to normal rhythm. He asked them if he was going to die. All he could think about was his family at home and how he didn't want to die and leave them behind. At that moment, all of the money in the world did not matter. Two months later the business went up for sale and it sold in one week for exactly what we were asking for it. So when we think we are in control of our own lives and our ways are better than God's, He will make sure you that know He is the one in control.

Chapter 6

Surrender Addictions & Strongholds

Going through my journey of redemption and salvation over the past 15 months, my choice of therapy was reading spiritual books about how God is our ultimate healer and Jesus is the answer to everything in life. Because I was a "baby Christian," these books were the only helpful thing in guiding me through my new-found life. I could not read and really understand the Bible yet because I still had not developed spiritual eyes to see what The Lord was saying to me through His word, so these books were my therapy.

Though I have come a long way with my healing, I still read spiritual self-help books today. My absolute favorite book in the entire world is the book I started reading the day I got saved, "When Godly People Do Ungodly Things: Arming Yourself in the Age of Seduction" by Beth Moore. After reading that book and many more written by her and other wonderful authors such as Tracie Miles, Pay Layton, Kimberly Jones-Pothier and so many more, I stopped spending $100 an hour in therapy with a Christian Counselor. Though she led me to read Beth Moore, I gained more knowledge and understanding of what I had gone through and what I would be going through with my self-help spiritual books. The books I read were of real people who experienced the same things I had. I could connect with the authors of those books a lot more than I could with the counselor since she hadn't experienced the same events in her life as I had.

In Beth Moore's book, "Praying God's Word," I love how she explains a stronghold.

"I have been educated in the power of God and His Word through the field trips of my own failure, weakness, and past bondage. This

book is a result of my unquenchable desire to share one of the most effective approaches to the liberated life in Christ that God has ever taught me: praying Scripture to overcome strongholds. Actually, I didn't discover what a vital part of my liberation this approach has been until long after I had begun practicing it. I suddenly realized it was no accident that I was finally set free from some areas of bondage that had long hindered the abundant, effective, Spirit-filled life in me. After the failure of all of my formulas, in my desperate search for freedom I cast myself entirely upon God. He faithfully led me to several deliberate practices that He knew would work. Stunningly, in fact, He also knew that He had given me the mouth to tell.

The key to freedom from strongholds is found, not surprisingly, in 2 Corinthians 10:3-5. "For though we live in the world, we do not wage war as the world does. The weapons we fight with are not the weapons of the world. On the contrary, they have divine power to demolish strongholds. We demolish arguments and every pretension that sets itself up against the knowledge of God, and we take captive every thought to make it

obedient to Christ."

    The apostle Paul, under the inspiration of the Holy Spirit,

did a masterful job of explaining it in 2 Corinthians 10:5.

Basically, a stronghold is any argument or pretension that "sets

itself up against the knowledge of God." The wording in the King

James Version draws a clearer image of a stronghold: "every high

thing that exalteth itself against the knowledge of God." "A

stronghold is anything that exalts itself in our minds, "pretending"

to be bigger or more powerful than our God. It steals much of our

focus and causes us to feel overpowered. Controlled. Mastered.

Whether the stronghold is an addiction, unforgiveness toward a

person who has hurt us, or despair over a loss, it is something that

consumes so much of our emotional and mental energy that

abundant life is strangled – our callings remain largely unfulfilled

and our believing lives are virtually ineffective. Needless to say,

these are the enemy's precise goals."

After many months of studying and understanding the power of a

stronghold, the only one who can break that stronghold is God. We are instructed to take our thoughts captive to Christ and replace Satan's thoughts with Jesus' thoughts. Meaning, read His word and make it relevant to my life instead of my own thoughts or those influenced by the enemy. For some people, the overwhelming power of a stronghold is broken immediately. Praise God! But the renewing of our minds and learning how to live without that stronghold ruling our life takes a little more time. A stronghold can only be demolished when we take all of our thoughts captive to Christ. You will overcome it with His divine power, but He may keep it as a thorn in your side to make sure you never have the power of that stronghold come upon you again. For my husband, the thorn in his side will always be anxiety. Though he has come a long way in his recovery from it, it is still something that The Lord does not let him forget about and makes sure that my husband will always be dependent on Him for times that he struggles with anxiety. The thorn in my side will always be the shame and guilt of my past. I know The Lord has forgiven me for what I have done and the sins I have committed. Though shame and guilt does not come from God, my dependence on Him is crucial. To ensure that

I depend on Him for everything, including working through my occasional dark times, He will not let me forget where He has taken me from and everything He has brought me through.

When I was going through postpartum depression after our first child was born, I could not handle the sadness. As I mentioned before, all I could ever think about was suicide and ending the broken life I had been living. I had to find a way to escape the demons inside me and the dark walls that were closing in on me. So I reached for the highly addictive prescription painkiller, hydrocodone. I had many surgeries up to this point so I had quite a few stashed away. I remembered how they made me feel when I took them; I didn't have a care in the world and whatever was making me sad before was not making me sad at all as long as I had this drug in my system. After just days of taking of them, the pills were starting to take hold of me and my life. I had multiple refill prescriptions of them so I continued to get them filled until the maximum was reached. When they were all gone I had to search the internet to see if I could get more. I thought I was going to lose my mind because I could not purchase any more. I was so desperate that I went as far as thinking about contacting a drug dealer in town just to get some. But once again, God was right there telling me that I had a daughter to take care of and the addiction had to stop. After a year of addiction, I was able to finally stop. It was not easy though; I had withdraws that led to vomiting and severe headaches.

Prior to my hydrocodone addiction, I had an exercise bulimia addiction. That is the life-controlling disorder that is completely controlled by food and exercise. It is a subset of the psychological disorder called bulimia in which a person feels the need to exercise in an effort aimed at burning the calories of food energy and fat reserves to an excessive level that negatively affects health. The damage normally occurs through not giving the body adequate rest for athletic recovery compared to exercise levels, leading to increasing levels of disrepair. If the person eats a normally healthy and adequate diet but exercises in levels they know require higher levels of nutrition, this can also be seen as a form of anorexia. I was married and attending college at this time, so when I was finished with class I would spend the rest of the day working out until it was time to go home. I counted every calorie that went in my mouth and every calorie that was expended through exercise. I never felt that I looked good enough or that I was thin enough. This goes back to the enemy's lies about having to please man and not God. Whether I was 115 pounds or 315 pounds, God loved and accepted me. But Satan loved to tell me differently. My husband loved and accepted me the way I was and this addiction was really starting to affect our marriage. He started to really worry about me and began to monitor my every meal, my workouts and my behavior. No matter how thin I was, I was still never happy or felt good enough. During this time I was also modeling and was hired to participate in country music videos. That is a terrible industry to be in if someone is struggling with eating disorders. I was constantly comparing myself to other women.

I have always loved fitness and became very interested in it at the young age of 15. I started lifting weights and working out pretty heavily through high school and college. I played one year of college softball and was approached by the college coach to play basketball, but with the way I struggled in school without distractions, playing college sports was not an option for me. So I worked out and exercised a lot. I was also going to school to be a Physical Education teacher so it kind of went with the territory.

I received my personal training certification in April 2013 in hopes that I could replace my teaching salary with training clients and fitness classes. I started teaching exercise classes and my business started growing from there. I continued training the following school year as well as teaching. I would teach at school during the day and then come home at night and teach fitness classes and train clients. I was literally working all day, every day and I never saw my family. I just wanted out of teaching so badly that I was willing to sacrifice my family life and my sanity!

I was still looking for happiness in all of the wrong places. Jobs, money, physique, personal relationships and approval from people. But that is not where true happiness lies; you will only find happiness and a life filled with wholeness in a life lived for Jesus Christ. Though I did not enjoy my career as a teacher that was not the reason for my unhappiness. In John 6:25 Jesus says, "Very truly I tell you, you are looking for me, not because you saw the signs I performed but because you ate the loaves and had your fill. Do not work for food that spoils, but for food that endures to eternal life, which the Son of Man will give you. For on him God the Father has placed his seal of approval." (NIV)

My husband and I were both working for earthly things; I was working for the answer to happiness and my husband was working for more money. But Jesus declared in the book of John, "I am the bread of life. Whoever comes to me will never go hungry, and whoever believes in me will never be thirsty." But we continued to be hungry and thirsty because of earthy things, not eternal life.

My personal training business started to really grow and so did my confidence in myself. Due to endless hours of training and working out, I started to get in the best shape of my life. I could not believe how wonderful and confident I felt; I had never had that feeling before. I wore clothes that I would have never worn before. Along with this "perfect level of fitness" lifestyle came a lot of continuous work and dedication. I never wanted my physique to go back to what it had looked like in the past, so my addiction and idol became working out many hours every day. It was an obsession that I lived for. But as with any other kind of addiction, it is not something that you can easily stop. Tell that to an alcoholic that can't stop drinking or a pornography addict that can't stop viewing pornographic images. When an addiction becomes who you are, it is a stronghold that Satan has on you and is relentless with it. Anything that is held higher than God is an idol and He will not stand for it long; He will allow you to be brought to your knees.

The compliments and attention was fuel to the fire. The more compliments I had and the more attention I was receiving, the more I had to work out. And not only was I obsessed with working out, but now I was obsessed with the food I was putting in my mouth. I was conscious of everything I ate. I lived on protein shakes, meal replacement bars and very little fatty foods. My entire life was literally engulfed in ME! It was about how good I looked, how good I felt, how successful my clients were doing because of

ME! Oh my friend, that is when my world began to come crashing down!

Scriptures about the dangers of having idols above God:

> • Exodus 20:3-4 "You shall have no other gods before me. You shall not make for yourself a carved image, or any likeness of anything that is in heaven above, or that is in the earth beneath, or that is in the water under the earth." (NIV)

> • Psalm 135:15-17 "The idols of the nations are silver and gold, the work of human hands. They have mouths, but do not speak; they have eyes, but do not see; they have ears, but do not hear, nor is there any breath in their mouths." (NIV)

> • Isaiah 44:9-12 "All who fashion idols are nothing, and the things they delight in do not profit. Their witnesses neither see nor know, that they may be put to shame. Who fashions a god or casts an idol that is profitable for nothing? Behold, all his

companions shall be put to shame, and the craftsmen are only human. Let them all assemble, let them stand forth. They shall be terrified; they shall be put to shame together. The ironsmith takes a cutting tool and works it over the coals. He fashions it with hammers and works it with his strong arm. He becomes hungry, and his strength fails; he drinks no water and is faint." (NIV)

• Hebrews 13:5 "Keep your life free from love of money, and be content with what you have, for he has said, "I will never leave you nor forsake you."

• Leviticus 26:1 "You shall not make idols for yourselves or erect an image or pillar, and you shall not set up a figured stone in your land to bow down to it, for I am the Lord your God." (NIV)

• 1 Corinthians 6:19-20 "Or do you not know that your body is a temple of the Holy Spirit within you, whom you have from God? You are not your own, for you were bought with a price. So glorify God in your body." (NIV)

• 1 John 5:21 "Little children, keep yourselves from idols." (NIV)

Chapter 7

Surrender Your Life – My Testimony

"We all have different problems, but we all have the same

problem solver"

There is a bit of repetitiveness in this chapter due to this entire

book being my testimony.

Ok, so now that I have told you how awesome God is, I am going

to tell you why He is so awesome. I can say this because I have

experienced first-hand the redeeming power He can do in

someone's life, and now you will too. As I've said, growing up religion was not talked about. I grew up in a small town in Michigan, 600 miles away from the Bible belt. When I moved to Tennessee at age 22 and saw how different the cultures were, I was definitely shocked. As a young girl, I attended church on my own but never had an intimate relationship with God. We never spoke of His name, unless we were taking it in vain. And we certainly didn't turn to Him when we faced struggles, problems or catastrophes!

The pit that lead to a life of destruction happened years ago as a child and I just kept digging it deeper as the years went by. Living in an abusive situation has lasting consequences that I was unaware of at the time. I just thought I was a kid who had a lot of problems who never made anyone happy and continuously let everyone down. After years of multiple failures, I just gave up! I thought, "Why bother? They are just going to be upset and yell at me any way." So at about 10 years old is when the masking began.

I started out with smoking, then self-mutilation, I cut myself with razors and knives on my arms and other body parts that were not easily seen. The pain I felt from the burn of the razor was a wonderful release. I focused on the physical pain that masked my emotional pain. From there I started drinking, that lead to stealing, lying and cheating. Then my friend, at the time, introduced me to the homosexual lifestyle – I was so confused because I was not attracted to women, I liked men. But the positive attention and approval I was receiving from them was overwhelming! Unfortunately, my pit has a lot of different labels on it. Going through life I did not realize how dark my life really was. I just figured that everyone lived a life like I did and kept it in secret. In public I had to push the pain and sadness down as if it didn't really happen. And after a while it just became part of my everyday life. I attended some counseling as a child, but they just thought I was a child who exaggerated everything.

I brought the baggage of my childhood into my marriage and my future family. As discussed earlier in the book, my husband and I both were searching for happiness and the meaning of life. I disliked my job and made it well-known to my husband that I was willing to take any job to leave the teaching job I was currently in. But what I didn't realize at the time, the teaching job was not the reason for happiness or unhappiness. My husband continuously told me that if I quit my job, we would have to sell everything we owned and live in a box on the side of the road. After a while, I felt like a paycheck to him and that was it. We were not going out on dates, spending quality time together, were not being intimate, he was sleeping on the couch and our marriage felt like a business partnership. When I started my personal training business, the positive attention I was receiving was overwhelming to me. I had never experienced that type of positive attention and experience in my life! At this time in my life, my relationship with God was far away from my mind and I was even further away from my marriage. Though we were struggling in our marriage and home-life, we had just started attending church together as a family, which we enjoyed and became more involved with church activities. I was still living life for me and enjoying instant gratification. I was in the best shape of my life and was receiving more attention from the opposite sex than I had ever experienced before. What I didn't understand was why I liked the attention so much because I loved my husband, I could never imagine myself marrying another man. I thought that when you got married, you never noticed another person's attention towards you. My husband is my soul mate, my best friend, and the best father in the world. What was going on with me? And this is when the Devil attacked. The attention from other men grew more and more and it eventually landed me in three affairs in three months. I will give you a minute to let that soak in….

An affair is not something that happens overnight; it is something that has brewed over months, if not years. Let me add something here about affairs that people don't understand much about unless they have experienced one. An affair does not have to only be sexual. There are emotional affairs that are extremely damaging to the other spouse as well. Anytime you step out of the marriage covenant, sexually or emotionally, it is an affair. In Matthew 5:28 it says, "But I tell you that anyone who looks at a woman lustfully has already committed adultery with her in his heart." (NIV) Even though each of my affairs lasted less than a month, and they were not all sexual, the damaging effects on our marriage will last a lifetime. The innocence of our marriage covenant has been forever violated.

Satan will find the tiniest crack in a marriage, takes advantage of our weaknesses and attacks! It happened so fast, though, that it seemed like it hit me out of nowhere. But it wasn't like I just met a guy off the street; Satan presented me with someone I knew and felt comfortable with. Someone that I had known for a long time. Something that started out so innocently in friendship, led to complete and total destruction.

My husband often asked me what I was thinking during the affairs. I told him that it felt as if I had a demonic spirit in me, like I was not myself. I was cold-hearted; I didn't care about anything or anyone. It was instant gratification that made me feel better for the moment. The problem was, that afterwards, I felt worse than I had before. So to make myself feel better again, I did it again. It was like I was a drug addict; I felt good on the high, but when I got off that high, I felt worse so I had to get high again. Though I wasn't saved at the time, I knew of Jesus and would cry out to Him "WHY is this happening to me?!?! I never asked for this! Make it stop!!" The problem was, I was so deep in sin that I could not get out. It felt like I was living in a fog, in a dark hole, all by myself with the Devil being my only friend. He told me that it would only happen once and that I could stop when I wanted to. That is not true, it is a spiritual warfare like no other. My spiritual side was pulling me one way and my human, sinful side was pulling me the other. The analogy I use to tell people what deep sin is like, it's similar to stepping in quicksand. You start by putting your toe in to "test" it. Then over time, your foot is submersed, and then your leg and soon your entire body is engulfed in quicksand and you are desperately crying for help out of it, but no one hears your cries. I actually stopped asking God to get me out of the affairs because I thought, "Forget it, if you can't get me out of these affairs (the quicksand), I will do it myself." Yeah, you can see where that got me. Sin is never satisfied, it will always take you deeper.

My husband has asked me multiple times how something like this could have happened. When you are in sin, you don't think about the consequences. Satan comes at us looking like everything we want, so we think. He does not come at us saying, "I am going to destroy you, your family and everything you have." If that was how sin happened, no one would do it. A person does not start doing drugs after being told, "You will lose your children, your spouse and your entire life you have worked for if you do this." NO, Satan tells them, "just try it once, you can stop at any time." I know it sounds crazy but it is almost like you are drunk. It's like you know what you are doing but you don't care. It feels like the Devil has his claws in you and you can't get them out. He knows your weaknesses and preys on them relentlessly.

I know that people may judge and say, "I can't believe she did that! I would never do that to my spouse!" Be careful my friend, I said the same exact thing just months prior to my affairs. But I have an easy analogy to help you understand how someone could easily find themselves in this type of situation. Let's say you are on a diet and you tell yourself that you are not going to eat a piece of chocolate pie, or whatever your weakness is. You have self-control and you have disciplined yourself so well that you are determined to not eat a piece of chocolate pie. It's been about one month on this diet and you are really struggling and craving a nice, rich and creamy slice of your favorite chocolate pie. Your spouse brings you home a slice of chocolate pie and you are not only craving chocolate that you haven't had in over a month, but you are starving and sick of eating salads and food that tastes like cardboard. Let's see how well you do when that piece of pie is placed in front of you and you are alone and free to decide whether you are going to eat that piece of pie or be strong and walk away from it...... what would you do? We can never answer that question until we are in that exact situation.

I was still so in love with my husband and that was something I was so confused about. I did not understand why I was doing what I was doing, while still in love with my husband. I always thought people entered affairs because they no longer wanted to be married to their spouse. But in my case, that was not the situation at all. Something in me was driving me further into darkness, and the double life I was living was spinning out of control. My husband and children were the people I never wanted to hurt, but they would be the ones I ended up hurting the most.

The day I told my husband was the scariest day of my life. I had no idea how he was going to react, what he was going to say, or if I would even be married to him by the end of the day. All I knew was that this secret was burning inside me so bad that I could not take it anymore. I voluntarily told him a week after I ended the affair. He did not find out through emails, he did not catch me texting, I was completely open in confessing the life I had been living. He was in complete shock, he did not suspect it at all. It was because I was living a double life, there was no evidence, whatsoever, about an extra-marital affair. The problem was, as I was telling him about the first two, I was still involved with the third. I ended the third one shortly after I told him about the first two, but I could not bear to see him hurt another minute. So I just buried that secret deep down in me until I was ready to tell him.

I was at the bottom of my pit, I had never been lower in all of my life. But I had nowhere to turn, no one to talk to. Here I am a broken woman beyond repair with absolutely NO spiritual guidance in my life whatsoever. Who was I going to tell that I had three affairs in three months!?!? One day I was home alone and wanted to end it all. I could not take the torture any longer. I took my husband's gun out of the night stand, but I didn't know how to load it, so that suicide plan didn't work. God had other plans for me. Praise God!

The absolute greatest day of my life was on October 2, 2014 in the backwoods of Madisonville, TN. My mother-in-law and I were sitting in the car while my husband and his dad were out looking at a backhoe to purchase for some property my husband was planning to develop. I was at the end of my rope, planning my next suicide attempt, when I asked my mother-in-law, "How does God ever really forgive someone for their sins? Like someone who had an affair, for example, how can God really forgive someone who has done that?" Then she said the most beautiful words I had ever heard in my life, "You just have to surrender your life to The Lord." And at that moment I turned around facing forward in the front seat of that car and looked up to Heaven and whispered to myself, "Surrender your life to The Lord, Surrender your life to The Lord..." and at that very second I felt the weight of the world lift off of my shoulders, for the first time in my life I REALLY saw sunshine. I felt as if I laid on the ground at the feet of Jesus and gave my life up to Him. I imagined myself laying there holding up a white flag telling Him I give up, I can't live like this another second! I felt a blind fold taken off my face, and experienced God breathing life into my lungs. It was an indescribable feeling! I still did not know what happened right then, but I remember driving home that day from Madisonville, TN feeling happy and free, although I still had no idea why. I did not understand the whole plan of salvation.

I went to bed those next few nights still not knowing what exactly happened that day in the car with my mother-in-law. All I remember was saying to myself, "*I hope this happy, free feeling never goes away.*" I woke up every day thankful that I still felt the way I felt on Oct. 2nd. After talking with some spiritual friends at church and reading Beth Moore's books, I realized that life-changing day was the day I got saved!!!! It may sound funny to those of you who have been raised in church and a Christian home; but when you have had no guidance in your life about salvation or the plan of it, you don't know how it is supposed to happen or how it is supposed to feel. As I was growing in my spiritual life and walking closer and closer to The Lord every day, I knew I had to tell my husband about the third affair but didn't know when. I had already told him about the first two but struggled telling him about the third one. Throughout this journey of our life, I have had people ask me, "Why didn't you just tell him about the third?" I ask them this simple question, "Have you ever dreaded telling your husband how much money you spent shopping?" Ok, multiply that by about a billion and you might start to have an idea why it is so difficult. A huge lesson my husband and I have learned through all of this is to never be judgmental; you don't know what you would do or how you would feel until you are faced with the same situation.

I continually asked The Lord to reveal to me when it was time to tell my husband. I asked God to present it to me and when He did, I would do it. The secret was burning in me, but I knew the Lord's timing is always perfect. From the time I was saved until New Year's Eve 2014 (approximately 3 months), my husband never asked about the third guy. My husband knew the guy and had been concerned about him but never asked me about him after I was saved. I never really felt The Lord convicting me to tell him until the time was right. On New Year's Eve, out of the blue my husband asked if I had ever had an affair with the third guy. And right there I knew, The Lord was telling me it was time to tell him. I felt the Lord's timing was perfect because if I were to have told him right after I got saved, he may not have believed that I really was saved. My husband needed to see the change in me to believe that I had really been changed and was a new person in Christ.

After telling my husband that day, The Lord was working on me to tell someone else. I was sitting at my mother and father-in-law's dinner table the next day and The Holy Spirit was convicting me to tell them. I have no idea why; my husband never told me I had to tell them. I did not *want* to tell them, which is something that no one would really be proud of telling anyone, but the Holy Spirit was telling me to tell them NOW! As I sat there with my heart pounding and tears flowing, I voluntarily told them what I had done. Telling my in-laws what I had done was, by far, one of the most difficult things I had ever done in my life. As I exposed my secrets, my guilt, my shame, and the embarrassment was more than I could handle. But I know that I was supposed to tell them because the Holy Spirit was guiding me, I never felt alone. I felt His conviction so strongly that day that I literally could not stand up from the dining room table I was seated at. He was not allowing me to leave that table until I had told them. Though it was difficult, it was a huge burden lifted off me and I was no longer holding on to that secret that was burning in me. The Lord was not only working in me to confess my hidden sins, but He was also working in my husband to tell me his unconfessed sins. After we arrived back home from his parent's house that weekend, my husband had a burning secret inside that he held onto for seven years. He told me that when our first daughter was born and we were experiencing the troubles and hardships in our marriage, he admitted to watching pornography multiple times. I had asked him back then if he had ever watched porn and he continuously told me no. So when I found out that he held this secret in for so long, I was devastated! He told me the reason he didn't tell me before now is because he thought I would leave him. I have forgiven him for keeping that from me for so long.

I never understood the difference between Godly sorrow and worldly sorrow until I experienced it myself. I experienced worldly sorrow before salvation and Godly sorrow after salvation. The bible clearly teaches us that there is a sorrow that is according to the will of God. In 2 Corinthians 7:10 the bible says, "For the sorrow that is according to the will of God produces a repentance without regret, leading to salvation, but the sorrow of the world produces death." What does this sorrow look like? Well

it first produces repentance which leads to salvation. Repentance is the act by which we realize we have offended a Holy and Righteous God so we turn from our sins, begging God for forgiveness and we turn to Him and His ways. Repentance is always focused on our sin's offensive attack on God and our desire to make that right. That focus is what separates godly sorrow from worldly sorrow. Godly sorrow is guilt over sin, guilt over offending and hurting God. Worldly sorrow is focused on us, it is feeling guilty because we got caught, or in my situation, because I didn't want my husband to leave me. It is a sorrow that is focused totally on our hurt, on how we have been offended and not treated fairly. Godly sorrow, however, ignores the offense of self and instead focuses on how God has been offended. Godly sorrow leads us to such a strong desire to make our repent of our sins and to receive forgiveness from God that we surrender to salvation with no regrets. How can we choose to follow Christ, forsaking self and our old way of life so quickly without any regrets? Simply because, we have realized just how horrible our offense against God was and how horrible His justice against that sin will be. When I told him about the first two affairs, I experienced worldly sorrow; after I got saved I experienced Godly sorrow. The difference between how I apologized before getting saved and how I apologized after getting saved, is as different as night and day.

After I got saved and told my husband about the third affair, I got down on my face at his feet and begged him for forgiveness. I had never cried so many tears in my life as I had in that time of confessing to what I had done. He was so sweet, he lifted me up and told me that no wife of his was going to beg at his feet. He told me he loved me so much and was willing to work through the mess we were now faced with. I have never in my life experienced the love from him as I had that day. Through the pain and suffering he was feeling at that moment, he was still lifting up my face and welcoming me with open arms just as Jesus did the day I fell flat on my face at His feet. However, with each decision we make in our lives, there are consequences. My husband and I are closer to God and to each other more than we ever have been. But, we struggle daily with the consequences of our sins. He has difficulty with trust and security, he has nightmares about what happened, and has daily triggers that the devil has a field day with. The consequences for me are the guilt, shame, and sadness as to what I have done. But I know that it is from the devil because Jesus took my guilt and shame and nailed it to the cross.

Since my husband and I revealed our past secrets to each other, our marriage has flourished. We have a new love and appreciation for one another. We realize what we both almost lost and we cherish every moment now with our children and each other. But it is nothing that we did to save our marriage. It has been the work of God in our lives. Since putting Him first in our house, marriage, and family, our entire outlook on life has changed. We no longer worry about the little things in life, we have no control over them anyway. We have dedicated our lives to God and will continue in sharing our powerful message of hope, reconciliation, and redemption that rose up from the huge mess that was in our marriage. We know from personal experience how broken and lost individuals and relationships can be. But we also know the power and depth of the redemption, grace, hope, mercy, and forgiveness God can bring to a situation that may seem hopeless. We continue to struggle today with the pain and memories of what happened, but with each passing day, the load gets a little lighter.

My life transformation has not just affected my life but my husband and children's lives as well. Before I was saved I was cold-hearted, selfish, angry, depressed, sad, irritable, lost, hopeless and in chains of bondage from my past. This past year since I got saved I live in peace, I have hope for a future, full of life, happy, joyful, content, patient, a heart full of love, forgiving, free of bondage, a relationship with God that I never thought possible, thankful, I worry less, and an outlook on life that I never even knew existed. I had always heard how "different" you feel after you get saved but I never understood it until now.

I hope that you or anyone else never has to go through the biggest trial of their lives in order to be brought to salvation as I did. But I will say this, even though my trial and journey through all of this was more than I ever thought I could handle, my salvation and relationship with The Lord makes it all worthwhile. There is no hope of going through life if you don't have Jesus. He has transformed my life from the train wreck that it was to the freedom of life that I live now. If people go through these extremely difficult times in their lives without Jesus, that may be why it sometimes ends in suicide; they can't live an empty, hopeless life any longer. When they live a life of no Jesus, they are living hopeless lives. The day you are saved He breathes life into you and it is life everlasting.

The abuse I experienced in my childhood continued after being married and having children of my own. Finally, on July 8,

2015, The Lord spoke to me and told me it was time to witness to them and break the chains of bondage I have been in my entire life. One of the most difficult, but very rewarding, things I have ever done was witness to my abusers. The moment reminded me of when God shut the mouth of the lion in the lion's den with Daniel. They stayed silent long enough to hear the words I spoke to them about the gospel of Jesus Christ. The most amazing thing about witnessing to someone about Jesus is, the words you speak are not your words. Matthew 10:19 says when you come up against your accusers, don't worry about what you are going to say, it will be said for you. The Holy Spirit speaks for you and through you. As I was witnessing, my husband began to cry tears of joy. He had never heard me say the words that I was speaking. When the conversation was over he asked how I knew all the words that I was saying. I told him that I didn't remember what I had said because it was not me speaking. I could have never spoken such eloquent words on my own as I spoke in that moment.

Since that day of breaking those chains of bondage that I lived in for 35 years, I have felt so free! I feel I can move further in my walk with The Lord, I feel I can freely speak about the abuse and not worry about what the abusers might say to me. I feel very comfortable about witnessing to anyone I need to and not having to be ashamed of my faith and what God has done for me. I don't have to answer to anyone any longer, I answer to God and only God. He fights my battles for me, I am just the vessel He uses.

Mark Batterson is another wonderful, Christian author and my husband and I have read a number of his books. In his new book, "If: Trading Your If Only Regrets for God's What If Possibilities," he states this passage that reminds me of the day I broke the chains of bondage with my past:

"God got Israel out of Egypt in one day, but it took forty years to get Egypt out of Israel. It happened at a place called Gilgal, 381 miles northeast of Egypt. The Israelites thought like slaves, acted like slaves. After all, it's tough to break the cycle after four hundred years of slavery.

Technically, the Israelites were set free at the exodus. Practically, it took forty years to fully exorcise their demons. It wasn't until they reached Gilgal that they finally left the past in the past. God said, "Today I have rolled away the shame of your slavery in Egypt." Sometimes it takes forty long years to bring closure to the feelings of condemnation. Sometimes you have to travel 381 miles just to get the past out of your present. But no matter how long it's been or how far you've traveled, God can still roll away your If Only regrets. It's never too late to be who you might have been. We'll get to What If, but every path to the Promised Land must go through Gilgal.

If you are in Christ, you are no longer defined by what you've done wrong. You are defined by what Christ has done right. You are a new creation, but sometimes it takes time for your new nature to become second nature.

God can deliver you in one day, but it may takes years to break old habits or build new habits. And for the record, the key to one is the other. If you want to break the sin habit, you'd better establish a prayer habit.

Jesus came to put the past in its place – the past. We need to leave it there."

In my situation, it took 600 miles and 35 years to bring closure to condemnation and to get the past out of my present. The beautiful thing about living for Christ is that He has made me a new creature and I am no longer defined by who I was in my past. Praise The Lord!

The following scripture is my most favorite scripture in the bible because I can relate to it very well as I have stated earlier in the book. I know I have been in that pit that David is speaking about – unfortunately one too many times. In Psalms 40:1-3 David talks about a pit that He was in and how God pulled him out of it and set his feet on solid ground.

"I waited patiently for the Lord;
he turned to me and heard my cry.
He lifted me out of the slimy pit,
out of the mud and mire;
he set my feet on a rock

and gave me a firm place to stand.

He put a new song in my mouth,

a hymn of praise to our God.

Many will see and fear the Lord

and put their trust in him."

This was a prayer from David to God when troubles arose. David's stress is from the sins that he committed. They are aggravated by the gloating of his enemies. The enemy has a way of reminding us of our past sins. That is actually what I am struggling with at this season of my life. Though I was saved Oct. 2, 2014, and I am washed clean by the blood of Jesus and I have completely turned my life around from the sin I was in, the enemy still continues to remind me of it daily! But when I stay in the word and keep my eyes focused on the sin-cleanser instead of the sin-accuser, I have a much more peaceful day. When I put on the full armor of God, the devil flees. I can relate to David in this scripture so much. How about you? Have you ever dwelled on your past and thought, "There is no way The Lord will forgive me for what I have done in my past. I don't deserve to be saved." Of course we don't deserve it, none of us do! Even on our best day we all fall short of the glory of God. The only one who deserves Heaven is Jesus Himself. But because of what Jesus did for us on the cross, we have an advocate with the Father and we can be forgiven of our sins and live for eternity in Heaven. David goes on praising God for the mercy and grace that He continues to show David as well as He continues to show me. The grace and mercy that is shown to us is given to us if we stay faithful and true to God. We can't make a mockery of what Jesus did on the cross for us. That grace and mercy is poured out to us when we live the obedient life that is set before us in God's word. David continues to tell how God put a new song in his mouth and how he will continue to sing God's praises. After I was saved from the pit, my entire outlook on life changed. My heart, my mind, my thoughts, my activities, everything! One thing that was a big change for me was my music. My entire life I had been a devoted rap music kind of girl. For me, it was, "the dirtier, the better." The day I was saved that all changed. I could not stand to hear that filthy language; I am sure that contributed to why I did the stupid things that I did. I can see now how music can influence your mind, actions, thoughts, and heart. What goes in is a reflection of what comes out. The Bible states in Matthew 12:34, "You brood of vipers, how can you who are evil say anything good? For the mouth speaks what the heart is full of" (NIV). But I see all of that now that I have had the veil lifted from my eyes. Praise God! Now my kids, my husband and I all listen to Christian music. It is so uplifting and positive and when you keep your mind in a positive state always focused on Jesus, it is hard for the enemy to sneak in.

The final part of that scripture is what I hope unsaved people will want to do; they may seek and fear The Lord and put their trust in Him. I am living the life God has planned for me and I pray for many friend's and family's salvation every day, and I have told them what God has done for me in my life. I know it is not my job to save them and I would never attempt to, but the good news of God is SO GOOD that you can't help but to tell everyone about it. I want everyone to experience God's grace, mercy and peace just as I have.

The Lord will get everyone's attention sometime in their life. As the Bible says, "No one can come to me unless the Father who sent me, draws them." So they will be drawn, but it is up to them whether or not they give their heart to The Lord and are saved. The easiest analogy I have for our invitation and free gift of salvation is when a person receives an invitation to a birthday party. They are invited to come, but it is up to them whether they will attend the party or not. No one will make them attend it just like God will not force salvation on someone. You have a choice to accept the invitation and attend, or deny the invitation. There are tangible ways in which those who are being drawn to salvation experience that drawing. First, the Holy Spirit convicts us of our sinful state and our need for a Savior (John 16:8). Second, He awakens in us a previously unknown interest in spiritual things and creates a desire for them that was never there before. Suddenly our ears are open, our hearts are inclined toward Him, and His Word begins to hold a new and exciting fascination for us. Our spirits begin to discern spiritual truth that never made sense to us before: "The man without the Spirit does not accept the things that come from the Spirit of God, for they are foolishness to him, and he cannot understand them, because they are spiritually discerned" (1 Corinthians 2:14). Finally, we begin to have new desires. He places within us a new heart that inclines toward Him, a heart that desires to know Him, obey Him, and walk in the "newness of life" that He has promised (Romans 6:4).

When we wait upon the Lord we receive four things: (1) He lifts us out of despair (2) Sets our feet on solid ground (3) Shows us where to walk (4) Gives us a new song of praise. Often we can't receive a blessing until we go through a trial of waiting. When we wait on the Lord and show that we trust Him and His plan, the reward will be given to us. In my seasons of sin, I waited for the Lord to take me out of the sin but He would not do that until I showed some work on my part. I asked Him long ago to get me out of whatever I was going through at the time; but until He saw that I was really ready to get out of it and give Him my all, He made me wait. And He is worth every minute!

When we are in the depths of despair is when we recognize we need a Savior. It is usually not when the money is flowing nicely, our jobs are tightly secured, our health is in tip-top shape and our family life is at its best. It is when we are in the midst of our mess. Yet many people fail to talk about the messy moments that lead them to the cross. And for that matter, the dark moments that follow salvation. We still have our moments of sorrow, pain, guilt, and shame. We are not *perfect* creatures before or after salvation, we are simply *redeemed* creatures after salvation.

You may be going through a trial right now. You may be the person that I was, still "riding the fence" on salvation. The bible states in Revelation 3:16, "So, because you are lukewarm-- neither hot nor cold--I am about to spit you out of my mouth" (NIV). You are either saved and producing fruit or you are not saved; you can't be in between. I thought I was saved but I was not living a life that produced fruit with evidence of salvation. It took me going through the biggest trial of my life; I almost lost my husband, my kids, my home, and my life! All the while, God was still there, waiting for me to get to the bottom of my pit so that I would be low enough to finally look up. As I said before, I always knew there was a God in Heaven and a man named Jesus who once walked the Earth. I always knew and believed that God existed and I always had some type of connection there with Him. But the scene looked like this: Here I am doing these sinful things living in the moment and experiencing instant gratification. Only calling on God when I really needed Him; a convenience God. Meanwhile, on the other side of the wall is Jesus sitting on a chair twiddling His fingers and patiently waiting for the doors of my heart to open to let Him in. I felt like there was a wall in between Jesus and I and we only spoke to each other through that wall because I did not want to break down that wall. I knew that if I broke down that wall completely, I would have to stop living the life of sin I wanted to live. But as I said before, He will allow trials and heartache to happen to you so you will turn to Him. When life is going great, people do not see the need for God. I find it interesting that people want us to pray to God for certain things in their time of need, but when everything is going great for them, they don't care anything about God. People think they are living their lives the way they want to live and they don't need God to come in and mess it up. So in order to get their attention and draw them to Him, He allows

Satan to enter their lives and mess it up.......bad!!!! A time that Satan likes to enter a person's life is when they have started to attend church, started getting life in order and have begun turning from a life of sin and are heading in the right direction toward God. But because they are not completely sold out to God, Satan still thinks he has a chance to destroy them. So he distracts, deceives, and divides that person from their spouse and family; and that is when the real destruction begins. If someone is already living in sin, Satan does not worry about them because he already has them. Sinners are not a threat to Satan because they are not working for God's kingdom.

So when Jesus calls you, please don't ignore His call. He is calling you to salvation because His plan is so much better than yours. Trust Him with your life, He will never let you down. He loves you and wants you to live life and live it abundantly. Surrender your life today – we all have different problems, but we all have the same problem solver.

I know many of you are wondering why and how I am able to be so transparent and honest about the shameful events that took place in my life. The truth is, it is not about what I have done. My entire ministry and testimony is not about the mistakes I have made, it is about what Jesus did for us on the cross. Myself and so many others are a testimony to what God can do to the most broken, lost, dark, confused people in the world today. God will restore the messiest of situations and offer us a safe place to process our doubts, fears, insecurities, struggles and failures. It is the sick who need the ultimate Healer, not the people who are well. Being a saved child of God does not mean that I am perfect and have it all together. It means that I admit that I am weak and in need of a Savior. Yeah, ya think? After reading seven chapters of my crazy life I think we can all agree on that!

Some scriptures on the importance of your testimony:

> • Luke 8:39 "Return to your home, and declare how much God has done for you." And he went away, proclaiming throughout the whole city how much Jesus had done for him."

• 2 Timothy 1:8 "Therefore do not be ashamed of the testimony about our Lord, nor of me his prisoner, but share in suffering for the gospel by the power of God."

• Revelation 12:11 "And they have conquered him by the blood of the Lamb and by the word of their testimony, for they loved not their lives even unto death."

• Psalm 66:16 "Come and hear, all you who fear God, and I will tell what he has done for my soul."

• 1 John 5:11 "And this is the testimony, that God gave us eternal life, and this life is in his Son."

Chapter 8

Surrender To God's Will For Your Life

My Ministry

It has been 15 months since I got saved and surrendered my life to The Lord. In this last chapter I am going to talk about how much He has done for me and my life and what happens when you give Him your life. One of the biggest things I learned from all of this, as I have said before, is that we are not in control of this life. So why not let go and let God take care of it for us? Do you know how stress-free it is not having to worry about what I am going to do tomorrow? He will open doors and close doors for you; you never have to shove a door open or slam a door closed. After I got saved in October, it was quickly put on my heart to write a book. Wait, what? Write a book? I didn't even like to write an email, how was I going to write a book? I barely passed English class in school, who was going to read a book that *I* wrote? Well silly me, it was not me writing the book, it was God using me to write what He has put in my heart. After many long prayers and requested signs from Him, I could not believe the email I opened up the next morning that was sitting in my inbox. It was an email from Proverbs 31 Women's Ministry titled, "Do you have a story to share? Attend the Proverbs 31 She Speaks Conference and share your story." Once again, God answered and He answered very clearly. I was so shocked that I stared at the computer screen for every bit of 2 minutes. She Speaks conference is held every year for women who desire to be authors and/or speakers in the ministry. The day I opened that email was the day I started writing this book.

It is funny how my husband and I had our lives all planned out. Remember the backhoe we went to look at the day I got saved in Madisonville, TN? The reason we went to look at the backhoe is because we were planning on purchasing 20 acres to put multiple real estate investment properties on. We would only purchase the property and move forward with the investment if we could have had the land perk for at least 10 spots. There were other houses around that area so we figured it would be no problem. To our surprise, the soil scientist told us that he could only find a couple spots that perked. My husband was devastated! This was only a few days after I got saved and I told my husband that The Lord has something else for us in store and that investment was not meant to be. I had complete peace about the situation. The very next day we drove by a commercial building that was for sale in a very busy, high-traffic area. We never thought we could afford it because of its fantastic location. We had a price in mind that we were not going to exceed, the sellers immediately came down $33,000, and we purchased the building at a very fair price. The Lord had better plans for us than we did. We made plans to put my gym there and due to the building being located in a different town, we decided to relocate closer to the building. That worked out perfectly because my in-laws lived about 15 minutes from there. We wanted to get a fresh start from the life we had lived in Lebanon, so we put our house up for sale that following March and made plans to move closer to Dayton, TN.

I was still personal training and running a very successful fitness business during this time of transition. In the meantime, The Lord had other plans for me. I started training for a full marathon and noticed hip pain. I prayed that I didn't have to have another surgery but if that was what The Lord wanted in order for me to focus more on our new relationship, then I knew that was in His plans. Sure enough, I had torn my labrum in my hip and was going to have to have another hip surgery. The Lord will literally do anything to get your attention! Hip surgery? Really!? But He knew that without me having an injury, I would still be training full-time and depriving myself from writing this book and growing closer to Him. This injury forced me to stop training and start my ministry. I told Him after He saved me, "Lord, thank you for saving me and saving my marriage. Because of what you have done for me, I will live the rest of my life serving you." And that is exactly what I have done.

I started writing this book in November 2014, and I have read over 25 self-help spiritual books since then as my means of therapy. I started reading the Bible, participating in numerous Bible studies, taught multiple Bible studies of my own and continue to grow my relationship with God. There is no way I could have done all of that if I was still personal training 8 hours a day in addition to being a hands-on mother and wife. I know that God planned for me to stop training, write a book and have a burning desire in my heart for ministry. Going from a self-centered, hard-hearted, fitness-obsessed, rebellious attitude type of person, only the work of The Lord could have transformed me.

We put our house up for sale that following March and sold it in 7 days to the very first person who looked at it for only $5,000 less than the list price. Later I found out that my husband had prayed that if the Lord wanted us to move to Southeast Tennessee, it would be awesome if we sold our house in a week. It sold in exactly one week. At the end of May my husband resigned from his teaching position and we moved to Southeast Tennessee.

My abusers were not happy about our move, because we were moving another two and a half hours away from them. The last and final episode happened on July 1, 2015. My abusers got really upset at me about something that did not warrant them to be upset, and I could not take the abuse and mistreatment anymore. I cried out to God louder and more sincerely than I had ever done before, He answered and answered big! The following day I wanted to spend time alone with God while reading one of my self-help spiritual books. I will forever remember this day as long as I live. I had begged God for years for this day to come, a word from Him to tell me exactly what I needed to do about my relationship with these people who have hurt me for so long. This sign and revelation came as I was reading a wonderful book titled, "Confessions of a Good Christian Girl: The Secrets Women Keep and the Grace that Saves Them" by Tammy Maltby. I was reading about a woman whose husband was abusing her. She continued to ask God to soften her husband's heart so they could reconcile and repair their marriage. One day she was crying out to God and begging Him for an answer. This happened to be exactly what I was doing on that day and this is what I read,

> *"Her devotions that day took her to Romans 9, which referred her back to the Exodus story: "For the Scripture says to Pharaoh: 'I raised you up for this very purpose, that I might display my power in you and that my name might be proclaimed in all the earth.' Therefore God has mercy on whom he wants to have mercy, and he hardens whom he wants to harden"* (vv.17-18)

As I was reading that, I went back to the Bible and read the early chapters in Exodus about how Pharaoh's heart was "hardened" against the Israelites. When Moses first went to Pharaoh to ask for his people's freedom and to let them go, the Egyptian ruler hardened his own heart. Out of pride and stubbornness, he made a choice to refuse Moses's plea. After this happened a number of times, the Lord himself stepped in. After all of the plagues, it was God who hardened Pharaoh's heart against the Israelites. So it was actually God himself who made the Hebrew's situation in Egypt worse and worse and increasingly miserable, until they finally made up their minds to leave on their own. As I continued, this is when the revelation smacked me in the face and I started crying as I read,

> "The Holy Spirit continued to tell the woman, *I want to take you out of your Egypt. But I have to make things worse so you'll want to go. I have hardened your husband's heart for your sake – so you will want to be free.*
>
> *Are you talking about divorce?* She whispered in her heart, dreading the answer. *I am talking about your heart*, The Lord answered. *I am talking about the part of you that is so accustomed to abuse, disappointment, and rejection that you don't even know what freedom is. But I am going to move you past that. Regardless of what happens in your life and your marriage, I want your heart free. I am going to take you to a place of safety and freedom. But you're going to have to trust Me every step of the way."*

Praise The Lord! I fell to the ground flat on my face, cried and screamed out to God thanking Him for that very clear answer I had been asking Him for so many years. I had been so accustomed to the bondage I had lived in that I didn't know there was a way out. And if there was a way out, how would I be able to see it? Sometimes God allows the situation we are in to get worse so we will be willing to let go. We will finally be motivated to leave what we know, and trust Him to take us somewhere better. I have never experienced freedom and peace as I have since breaking free from that abuse.

When we moved to Southeast Tennessee we went "church shopping" for a few weeks and we were instantly hooked on a church in Cleveland, TN. The church was great! The music was awesome, the preaching was biblical and the people made us feel so welcome. Right away we were plugged into a Sunday school class that was designed specifically for married couples for our age group and our daughters were attending classes for their age group.

About three months after attending church, our Sunday school teacher asked us to teach class. *Ummmmmm, what? Teach Sunday school? Do these people really know who they are talking to? If they knew my past they would know that I am not worthy enough or qualified to teach God's word.* But I knew if The Lord called me into ministry, I had to answer this calling, no matter how scary it seemed to be. The Lord doesn't call the qualified, He qualifies the called. Prepared and ready to teach, my husband and I taught that Sunday school class with confidence and boldness that could have only come from The Lord. We had the class of 50 people in a great discussion and the experience was not scary at all. Especially with the combined 26 years of teaching experience between my husband and I, speaking and teaching was not foreign to us. At the conclusion of the class we taught, our Sunday school teacher said, "We would like you to share your testimony." It was a statement I'd been praying to hear for a year. Praise God! I was so nervous yet so excited, all at the same time. This would be the very first time we had ever shared our testimony. Our lives would be exposed to over 65 people we barely knew! But with much work and prayer, we shared it and to God be all the glory!

After giving our testimony, doors to other opportunities began to open. We were asked to give our testimony to a young, married couple's class, then to another church, then another and another. Not only do we speak to groups of people, but we have also been asked to mentor couples going through the same types of situations. Revelations 12:11 "They triumphed over him (Satan) by the blood of the lamb and the word of their testimony." (NIV) Our testimony is exactly what it is, a testament of what God has done for us in our lives. When you tell your story, you never know who you are helping. We were not saved and restored to be silent. My husband and I have dedicated our lives to helping broken marriages and relationships and telling what God can do to the most traumatic situations. Not many couples can make it through one affair, God helped us make it through three.

It is unbelievable how broken this world is. People hide their secrets and lies behind closed doors making everyone believe that everything in their marriage and in their life is fine. It pains me to hear stories from other women who are going through this with their husbands, as well as other problems, addictions, abuse and emotional troubles. But since I came out with my story, many people have felt comfortable to tell me their story. That is exactly why I answered the call to go into ministry. I want my story of hope and redemption to help others through their trials and tribulations by seeing that Jesus offers forgiveness and restoration by His work on the cross. I saw a post on social media one day that said, "Be the person who you needed in your time of need." That post really struck a chord in me – that is exactly what I want to do. I want to be the person to other people who I needed in my time of desperation. God truly turns a mess into a message, a trial into a testimony, makes brokenness whole, and a sinner into a saint.

I am looking forward to telling my story to more people wherever the Lord leads me. I don't know what The Lord has planned for me tomorrow or even next year, but the path He leads me to take is the path that I will follow. I have not been in charge of this life and I have never had control to begin with, so I just surrender each day to Him to see where He takes me next. Each morning I start my day out with my cup of coffee in-hand seated in my "prayer chair." My prayer chair is where I do my best speaking. I sit alone in silence with The Lord and ask Him what He wants me to do next. Sometimes I hear it loud and clear and sometimes I struggle to hear a whisper. But regardless, I know He is there. I read the bible every day for an hour to make sure I keep the armor of God on me and sword of the Spirit sharpened. Because we never know when the enemy will attack and we must be ready to face our next battle and have the confidence to overcome it.

I am so excited to know that God will continue to use me as a vessel to help others get out of the hell they are living in, just as He snatched me out of mine. I never imagined in a million years that I would hunger and thirst for His living water. It reminds me of one of my most favorite passages in the Bible when Jesus encounters the Samaritan woman at the well. Jesus shared with this woman about a different kind of water, the living water. Jesus said to her in John 4:13-14, "Everyone who drinks of this water will be thirsty again, but whoever drinks of the water that I will give him will never be thirsty again. The water that I will give him will become in him a spring of water welling up to eternal life." (NIV) The woman at the well tells Jesus to give her this living water He is speaking of. Jesus tells her to go tell her husband about it and she told Him that she didn't have a husband, but rather she had five and the man she is living with now is not her husband. Jesus knew the mess this woman was living in. He knew the living water He had to offer her was of no value to her until she admitted to the sin she was committing. He did not call her out to condemn and judge her. Rather He showed her how desperately she needed this living water He was offering to her. Grace and mercy met her in her pit of darkness and the encounter with Jesus forever changed her life. She didn't bury her guilt and shame and return to her life of sin. John 4:28-29 tells us, "The woman left her water jar and went away into town and said to the people, 'Come, see a man who told me all that I ever did. Can this be the Christ?'" This same woman who went to the well in the heat of the day to avoid the judgment of other people, ran to tell others about her beautiful meeting with Mercy. The same meeting with mercy that happened to the

Samaritan woman was the same mercy that I met my final day in that pit. I had no idea that God would put this passion and drive in me to go into ministry to help other people. I hated to read in school as well as throughout adulthood, until I got saved. Now here I am writing a book, speaking to groups of people about the redemptive power Jesus uses to change people, I am already looking forward to writing my next two books and continue teaching multiple Bible studies! Where in the world did that come from? It can only come from God. Working out and exercising used to be my therapy. Though I still enjoy working out and I can get a little irritable when I can't, but reading and writing are my means of therapy now. Since I started reading self-help spiritual books and spend each day in prayer, I haven't spent one more dollar on a counselor because God is the ultimate counselor, and it's free! I am not saying a counselor isn't helpful, because they are. I know many great Christian counselors who have helped counsel people and marriages in their desperate time of need. I, personally, have witnessed first-hand that God has the answers to all of your problems. Take time each day to spend quiet, quality time in His presence and seek His face to answer the many questions in your life.

If we are to move further on with our faith, we must recognize the priorities and idols in our life. We must examine our hearts and lives on where our priorities lie. Don't doubt for a second that you don't have an idol; we all do on this side of Heaven. The enemy is always trying to convince you of putting anything *but* God at the center of your life. If you are not sure, reflect on your life and ask yourself: *What do I think about the most? Where do I put most of my efforts? What do I talk about the most? What defines who I am?* Do whatever it takes to reorder your priorities and remove the idols that have taken over your heart.

A true encounter with God will forever change your life. It will take you from the depths of despair and will leave you wanting to shout from the mountain-top. He has taken my brokenness and made it beautiful. He has taken my guilt and shame and nailed it to the cross. He has taken my sins and has thrown them into the sea of forgetfulness. He has closed the doors of yesterday because I no longer live there and has opened the doors of my tomorrow. Won't you join me in living a life free of despair and shame that has been lifted off of us by nail-scarred hands of love? Then tell everyone how God has broken the chains of bondage you had lived in for so long.

I have written this book to tell you that whatever you are going through right now, life can be good again. It won't happen overnight and may not happen in a few months. It may take a while to trust again, forgive and heal the deep wounds that have left a scar for life. My husband and I are living proof that with God, time, forgiveness, mercy, and grace, it *can* happen. I hope and pray that my story has inspired you to believe and encourage you to start walking in a new direction. Because what Satan meant for evil, God meant for good.

The ABC's Of Salvation

Are you sitting in the position I was all of those years thinking, "How do I get this peace and freedom that other people have? How can someone be saved?" According to the Bible, God draws everyone to Him. It is our responsibility to accept this drawing. He will convict your heart, but it is up to you to acknowledge this conviction or deny it. Here is an easy way to understand how salvation happens:

A – Admit you are a sinner and in need of a Savior.

B – Believe that Jesus died on the cross for your sins.

C – Confess that Jesus is the Lord and Savior of your life.

God says in order to go to Heaven, you must be born again. In John 3:7, Jesus said to Nicodemus, "You must be born again." You may be saying, "But I am a good person! I have not committed crimes or been to jail? Surely God will not let a good person like me go to Hell?

Unfortunately, there are a lot of "good" people in Hell who did not ask Jesus into their heart and make Him The Lord of their lives. In the Bible, God gives us the plan of how *to be born again*, which means *to be saved.* His plan is simple! You can be saved today. How? First, you must realize you are a sinner. "For all have sinned, and come short of the glory of God" (Romans 3:23). Because you are a sinner, you are condemned to death. "For the wages [*payment*] of sin is death" (Romans 6:23). This includes eternal separation from God in Hell. " . . . it is appointed unto men once to die, but after this the judgment" (Hebrews 9:27). But God loved you so much He gave His only begotten Son, Jesus, to bear your sin and die in your place. " . . . He hath made Him [*Jesus, Who knew no sin*] to be sin for us . . . that we might be made the righteousness of God in Him" (2 Corinthians 5:21).

Jesus had to shed His blood and die. "For the life of the flesh is in the blood" (Lev. 17:11).

" . . . without shedding of blood is no remission [*pardon*] of sin" (Hebrews 9:22).

" . . . God commendeth His love toward us, in that, while we were yet sinners, Christ died for us" (Romans 5:8).

Although we cannot understand how, God said that my sins and your sins were laid upon Jesus and He died in our place. He became our substitute. It is true. God cannot lie. "God . . . commands all men everywhere to repent" (Acts 17:30). This repentance is a change that takes place in your heart and your mind. When you repent of your sins, you TURN AWAY from those sins, never to return to them. In Acts 16:30-31, the Philippian jailer asked Paul and Silas: " . . . 'Sirs, what must I do to be saved?' And they said, 'Believe on the Lord Jesus Christ, and thou shalt be saved . . . .' " Simply believe on Him as the one who bore your sin, died in your place, was buried, and whom God resurrected. His resurrection powerfully assures that the believer can claim everlasting life when Jesus is received as Lord and Savior of their life. "Yet to all who did receive him, to those who believed in his name, he gave the right to become children of God" (John 1:12). "For whosoever shall call upon the name of the Lord shall be saved." (Romans 10:13). *Whosoever* includes you. *Shall be saved* means not maybe, nor can, but *shall be saved.* Surely, you realize you are a sinner. Right now, wherever you are, repent; lift your heart to God in prayer. In Luke 18:13, the sinner prayed: "God be merciful to me a sinner." Just pray: *"Oh God, I know I am a sinner. I believe Jesus was my substitute when He died on the Cross. I believe His shed blood, death, burial, and resurrection were for me. I now receive Him as my Savior. I thank you for the forgiveness of my sins, the gift of salvation and everlasting life, because of Your merciful grace. Amen."*

Just take God at His word and claim His salvation by faith. Believe, and you will be saved. No church, no good works can save you. Remember, God does the saving. All of it! God's simple plan of salvation is: You are a sinner. Therefore, unless you believe on Jesus who died in your place, you will spend eternity in Hell. If you believe on Him as your crucified, buried, and risen Savior, you will receive forgiveness for all of your sins and His gift of eternal salvation by faith.

You might be saying, "Surely, it cannot be that simple."

Yes, it's that simple! It is scriptural. It is God's plan. My friend, believe on Jesus and receive Him as Savior today. If His plan is not perfectly clear, read this over and over, without laying it down, until you understand it. Your soul is worth more than all the world. "For what shall it profit a man, if he shall gain the whole world and lose his own soul?" (Mark 8:36).

Be sure you are saved. If you lose your soul, you miss Heaven and lose all. Please! Let God save you this very moment. God is giving you the gift of eternal life if you will just surrender your life to The Lord and make Him The Lord of your life. If not, YOU are choosing Hell. God will never SEND anyone to Hell, it is a person's choice to go to Hell when they do not ask Jesus into their heart. God's power will save you, keep you saved, and enable you to live a victorious Christian life. "No temptation has overtaken you except what is common to mankind. And God is faithful; he will not let you be tempted beyond what you can bear. But when you are tempted, he will also provide a way out so you can endure it." (1 Corinthians 10:13).

Do not trust your feelings. They change. Stand on God's promises. They never change. After you are saved, there are three things to practice daily for spiritual growth:

1. Pray -- you talk to God.

2. Read your Bible -- God talks to you.

3. Witness -- you talk for God.

You should be baptized in obedience to the Lord Jesus Christ as a public testimony of your salvation, and then unite with a Bible-believing church without delay. "Be not thou therefore ashamed of the testimony of our Lord . . . ." (2 Timothy 1:8) "Whosoever therefore shall confess [*testify of*] Me before men, him will I confess also before My Father which is in heaven" (Matthew 10:32).

My final words to you are this. No matter who you are, what background you came from, where in the world you live, what you have done, whether you are male or female, or the color of your skin. You were created to live a life that is pleasing to The

Lord. Do not worry about pleasing man on earth, you will fail them as they will fail you. It is never too late to turn your life around and live every day to the fullest. My prayer for this book is for it to be used as a tool for all of us to look at our messy lives and rediscover or discover for the first time, God's grace, mercy and redemptive power. Because remember, we all have different problems but we all have the same problem solver.

Self-Reflection Questions

*

Now that we are friends, it is time for me to ask you some very important questions for you to reflect on. Some may relate to you and some may not. Take your time and answer them to the best of your ability.

How has abuse affected your life? _____

_____

Reflecting on your daily routine, do you recognize an activity or "thing" that could be a potential idol in your life? _____

_____

*I do not own the rights to this picture

Do you have a friendship / relationship with someone of the opposite sex that could cause a possible marital problem in your future?_____

Give examples of ways you've searched for happiness in all of the wrong places _____

_____

Define what salvation means to you _____

_____

Explain your moment of salvation. Was it different than any other day in your life? _____

_____

_____

Did you experience a true transformation in your life after you got saved? _____

_____

When you are faced with a time of struggle in your life, what/who is the first thing/person you turn to? _____

_____

If you are saved, could someone differentiate between you and an unsaved person? Do you have evidence of bearing fruit? (*2 Corinthians 6:17 "Therefore, come out from among unbelievers, and separate yourselves from them, says the LORD. Don't touch their filthy things, and I will welcome you."*)_____

_____

If you are saved, do you continue to indulge in the sinful things that you did before you got saved? What sacrifices have you made for The Lord? _____

_____

Follow Shannon on Facebook at "Surrender Ministries For Women with Shannon Wright"

Visit Shannon's blog www.surrenderministriesforwomen.com

Contact Shannon - surrenderministriesforwomen@yahoo.com

References

- Beth Moore, *Praying God's Word: Breaking Free from Spiritual Strongholds* (B&H Publishing. Nashville, TN 2009)

- Tracie Miles, *Your Life Still Counts: How God Uses Your Past to Create a Beautiful Future* (Bethany House Publishers. Bloomington, MN 2014)

- Tammy Maltby, *Confessions of a Good Christian Girl: The Secrets Women Keep and the Grace that Saves Them* (Thomas Nelson. Nashville, TN 2007)

- Mark Batterson, *If: Trading Your If Only Regrets for God's What If Possibilities* (Baker Publishing. Grand Rapids, MI 2015)

- The NIV Study Bible (Zondervan. Grand Rapids, MI 2011)